Cécile CHAMINADE
SELECTED COMPOSITIONS
FOR PIANO

A Kalmus Classic Edition

K 02185

CONTENTS

Sérénade, Opus 29 4
Minuetto, Opus 23 9
Air de Ballet, Opus 30 15
Pas des Amphores, Opus 37, No. 2 25
Callirhoë, Opus 37, No. 4 30
Lolita, Opus 54 35
Scarf Dance, Opus 37, No. 3 41
Pièce Romantique, Opus 9, No. 1 44
Gavotte, Opus 9, No. 2 46
Pierrette, Opus 41 49
La Lisonjera, Opus 50 54
La Morena, Opus 67 62
Les Sylvains, Opus 60 68
Arabesque, Opus 61 74
Valse-Caprice, Opus 33 80
Danse Pastorale, Opus 37, No. 5 90
Arlequine, Opus 53 97

Cécile-Louise-Stéphanie Chaminade was born in Paris on August 8, 1861. From an early age she showed signs of rare musical ability. At the age of eight she composed sacred music that won the attention of Bizet, who predicted a brilliant future for her. She studied with LeCouppey, Savart, Marsick, and Godard and made her piano concert debut at the age of eighteen. She soon became famous as a composer. Her compositions were so strong that, in ignorance, several critics referred to her early publications as the work of a man. Musician, author, and poet Ambroise Thomas said after a performance of one of her works, "This is not a woman who composes, but a composer who is a woman." This quickly put Chaminade in the circle of famous musicians of the time.

Her principal work, *Callirhoë*, a ballet-symphony, was premiered in 1888 in Marseilles, and performances of other orchestral and operatic works soon followed. In addition to orchestral and stage works, a great deal of her musical output was for piano. Her major works were often performed across Europe and in America. All of her compositions show expressive melody, accentuated by sparkling rhythms, and extensive use of chromaticism combined with musical values produces novel, graceful effects. Her vocal literature was in great demand by concert artists of her day, and she often continued performing her own piano compositions as a touring concert pianist. Chaminade was also highly regarded as a conductor in concerts in Paris, where she held a governmental appointment as Officer of Public Instruction.

Chaminade died in Monte Carlo on April 18, 1944. Her piano compositions survive her and continue to be used in lessons and recitals.

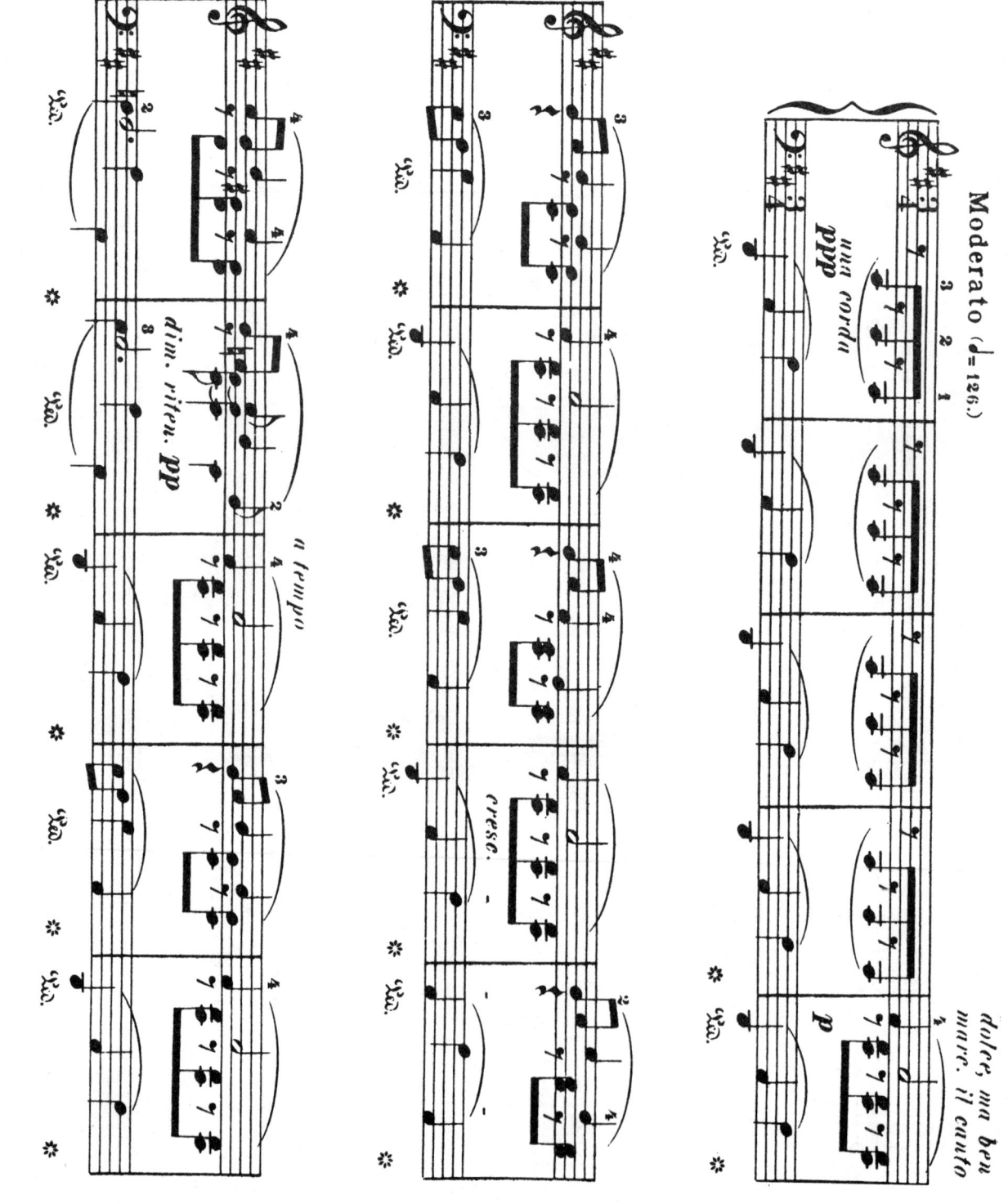

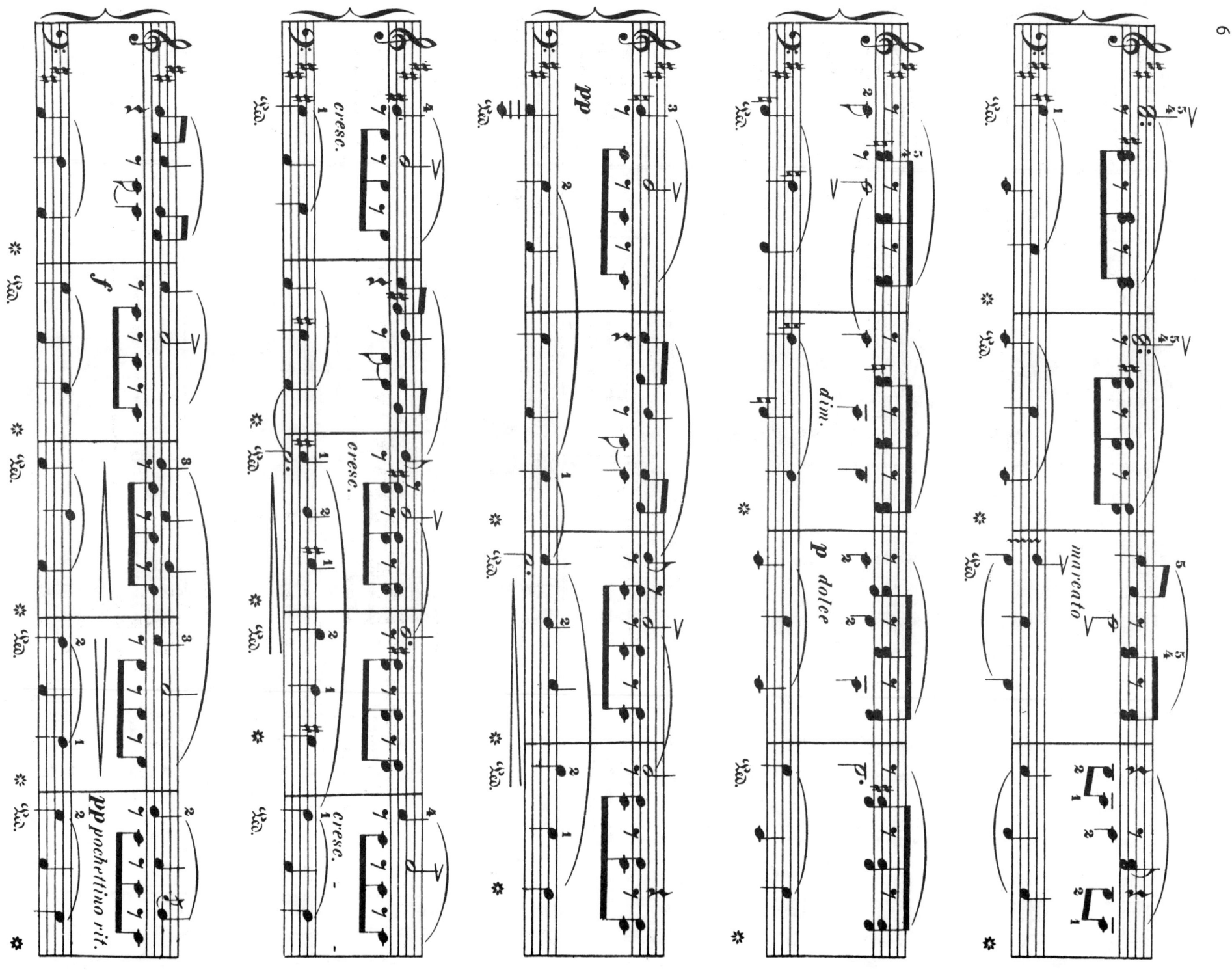

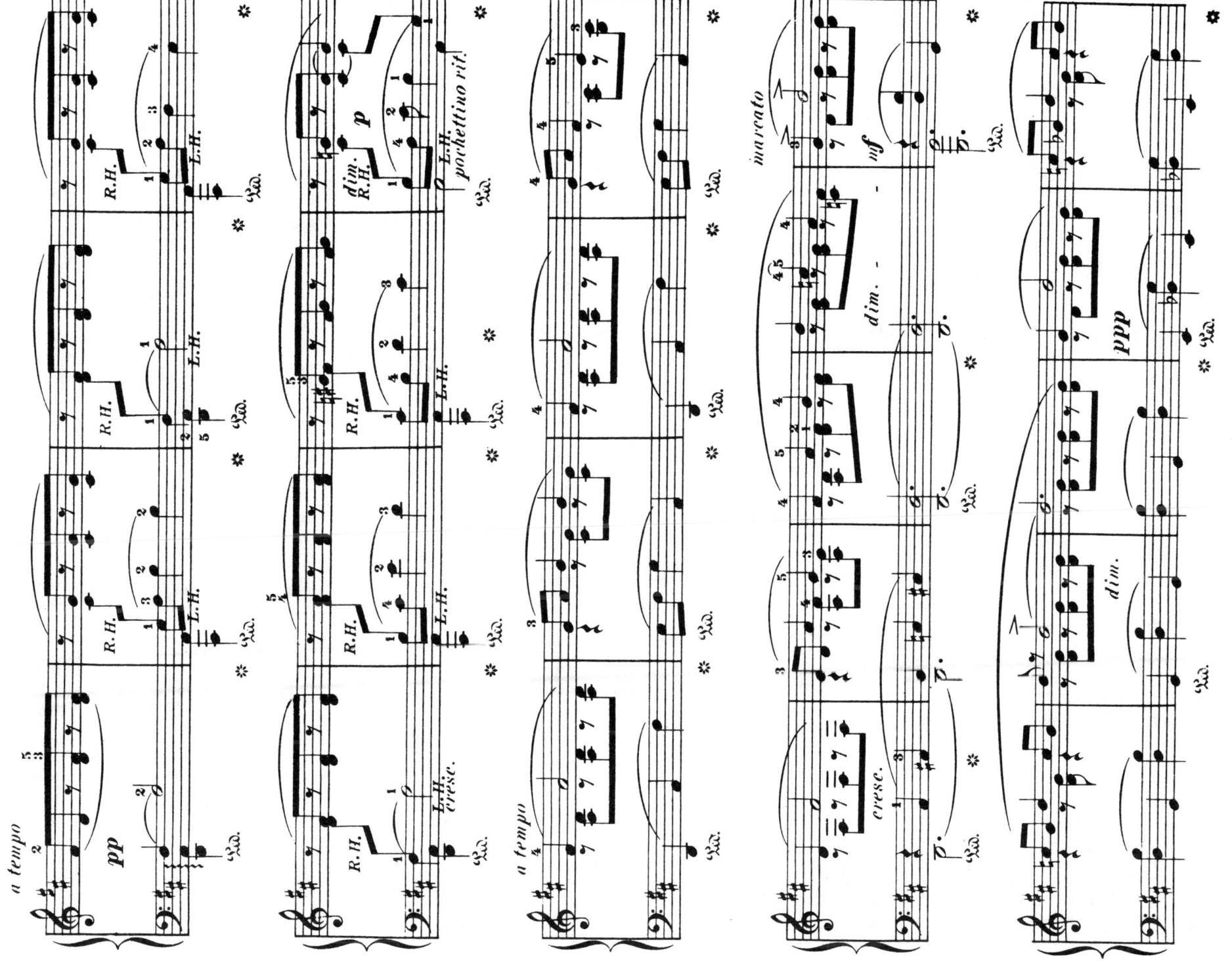

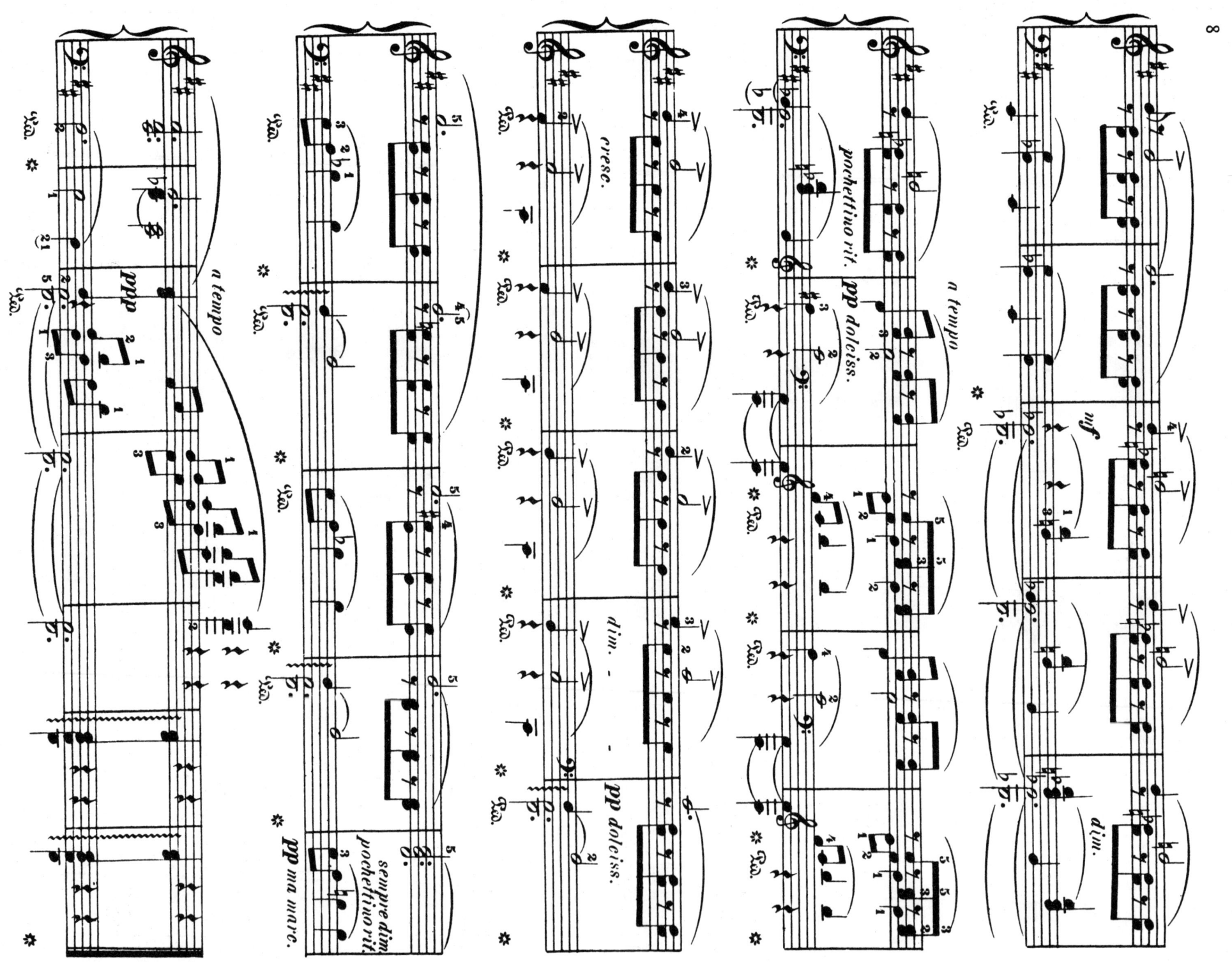

MINUETTO
Opus 23

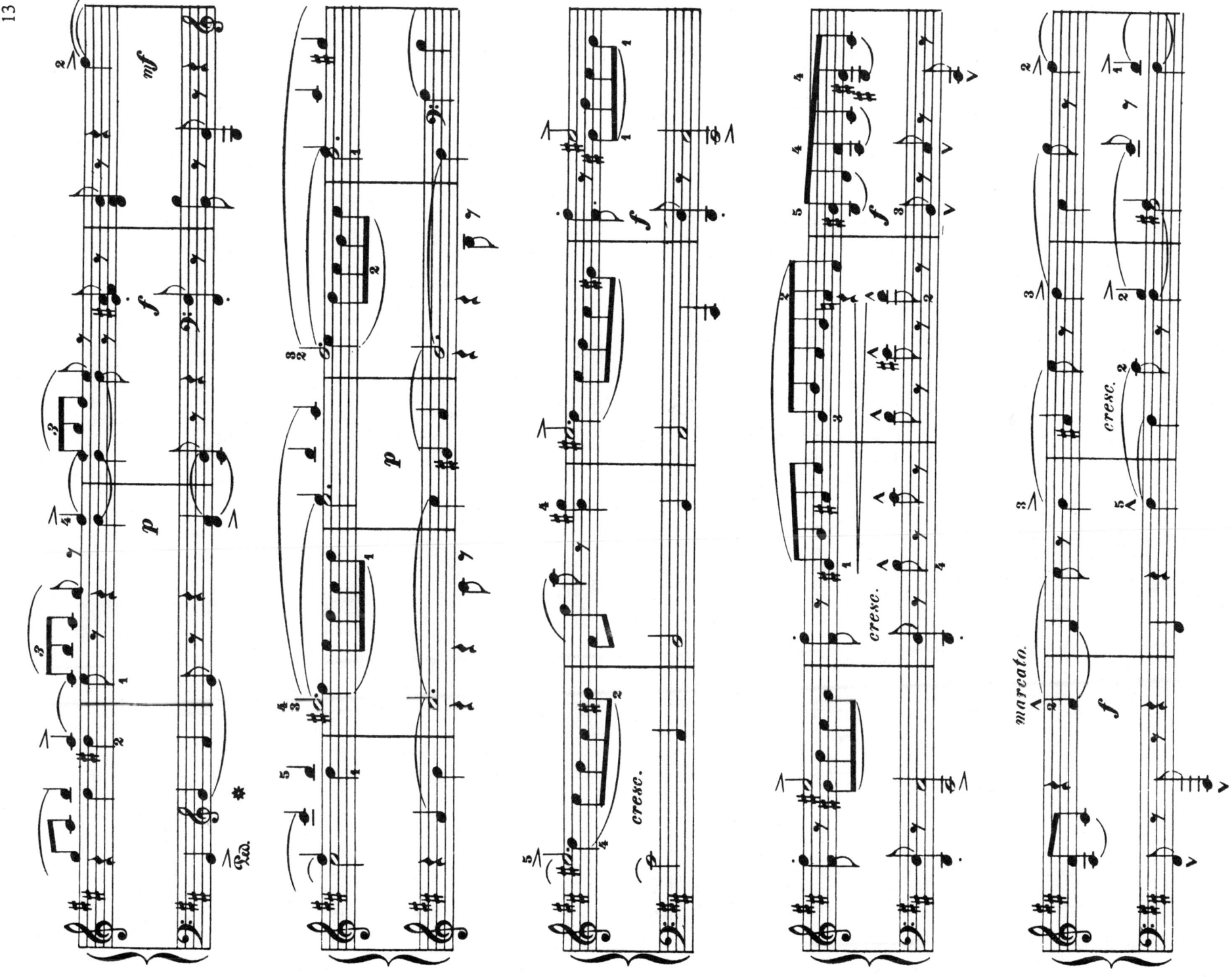

AIR DE BALLET
Opus 30

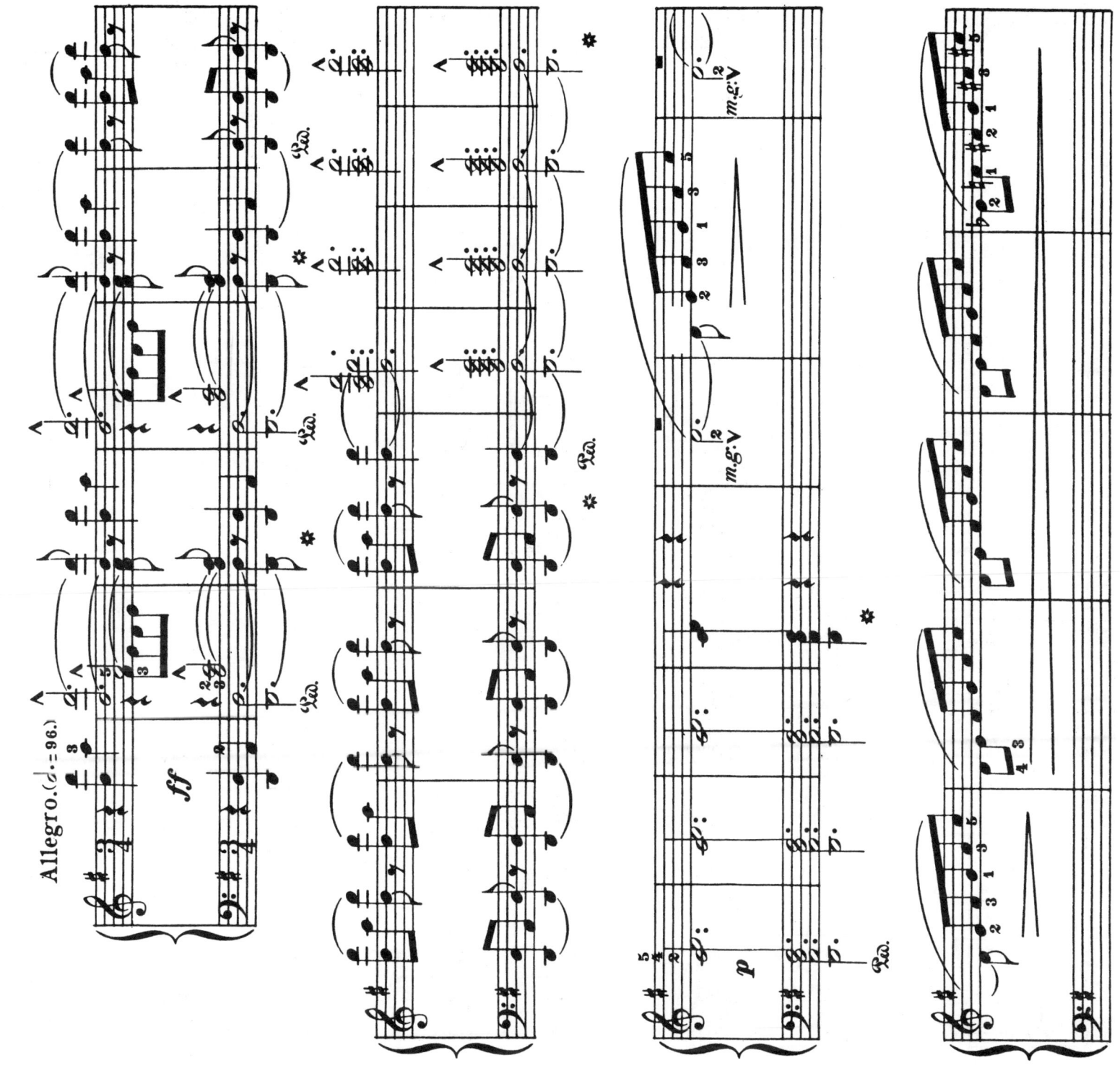

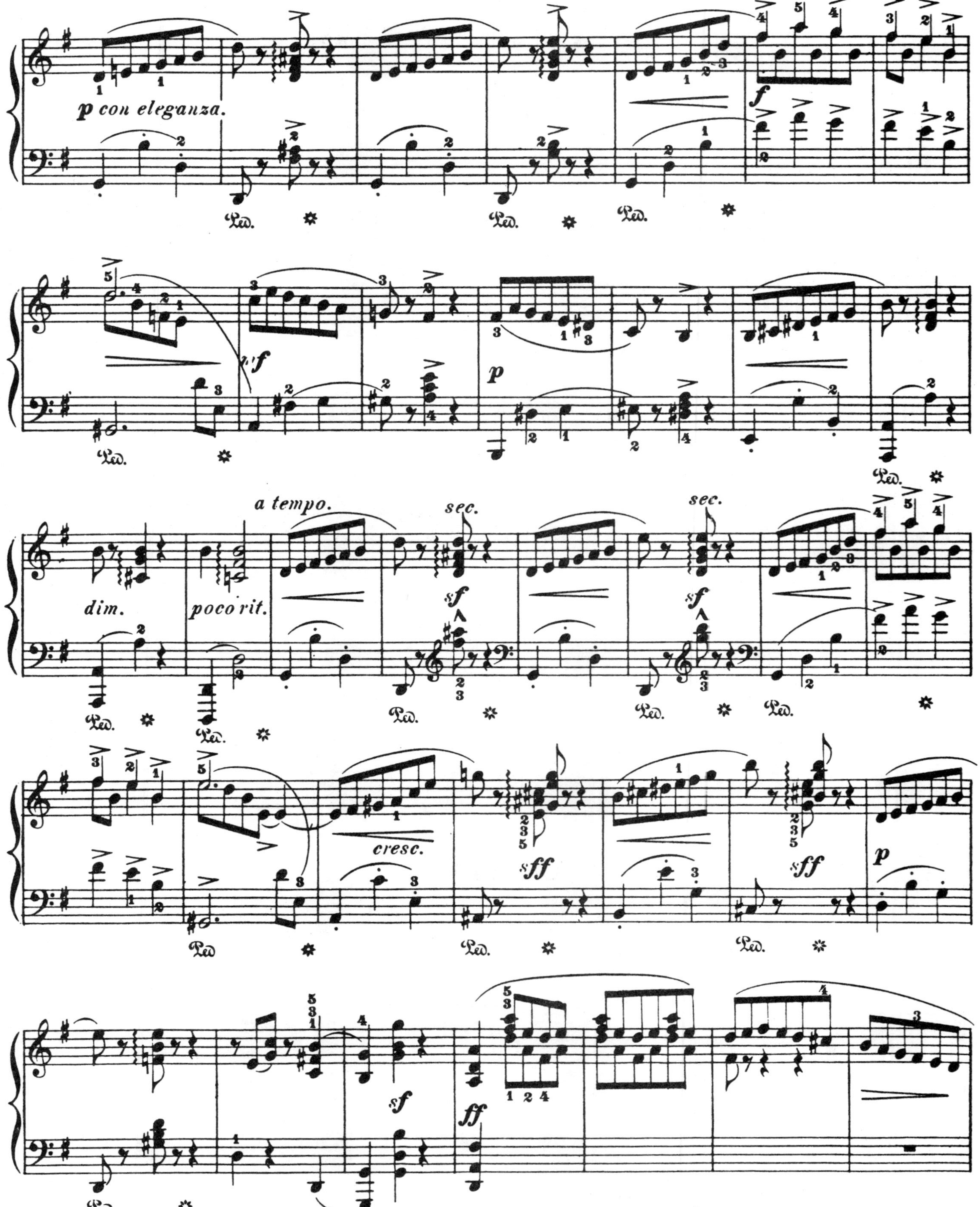
p con eleganza.
f
sf
p
a tempo.
sec.
sec.
sf
sf
dim.
poco rit.
cresc.
sff
sff
p
sf
ff

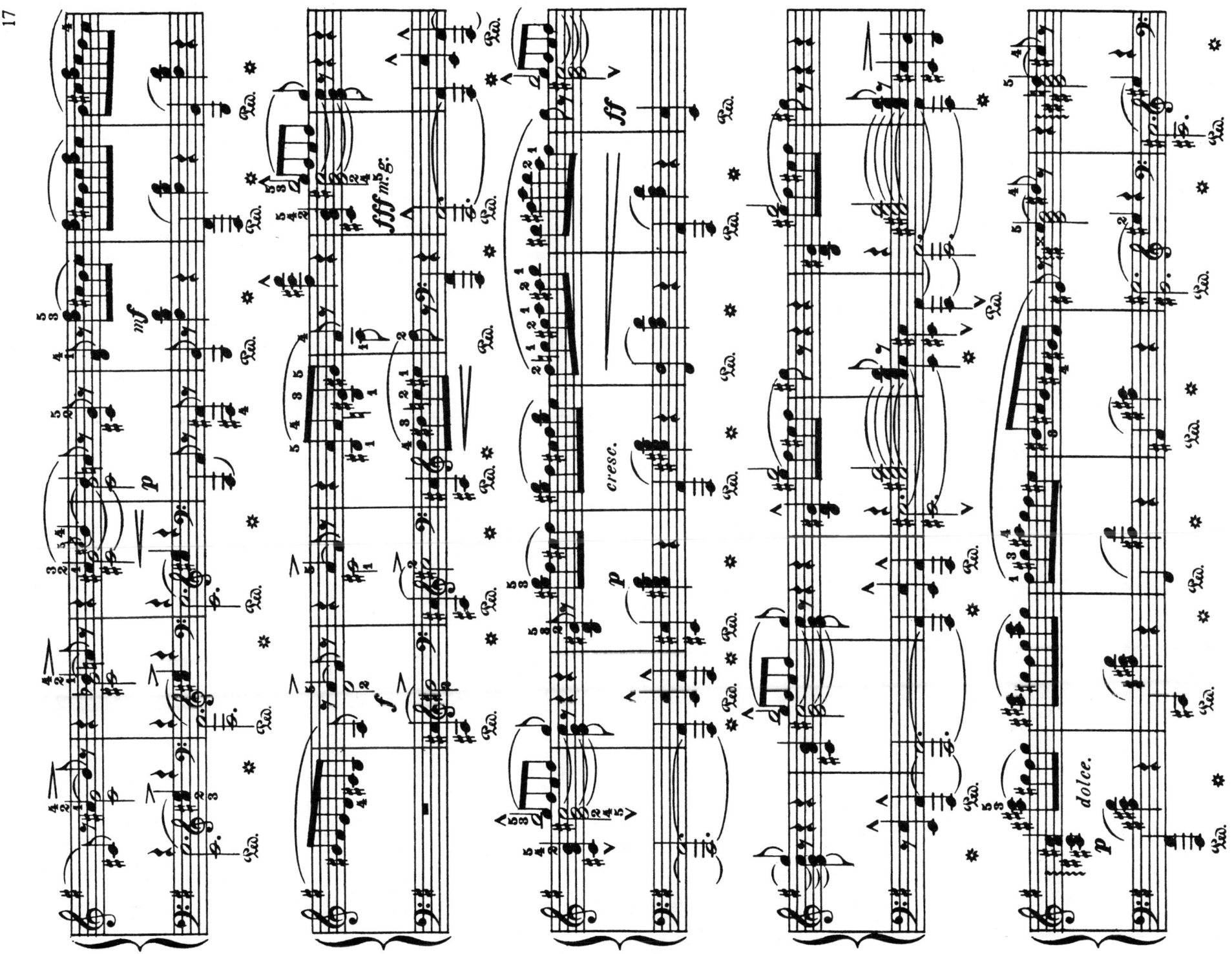

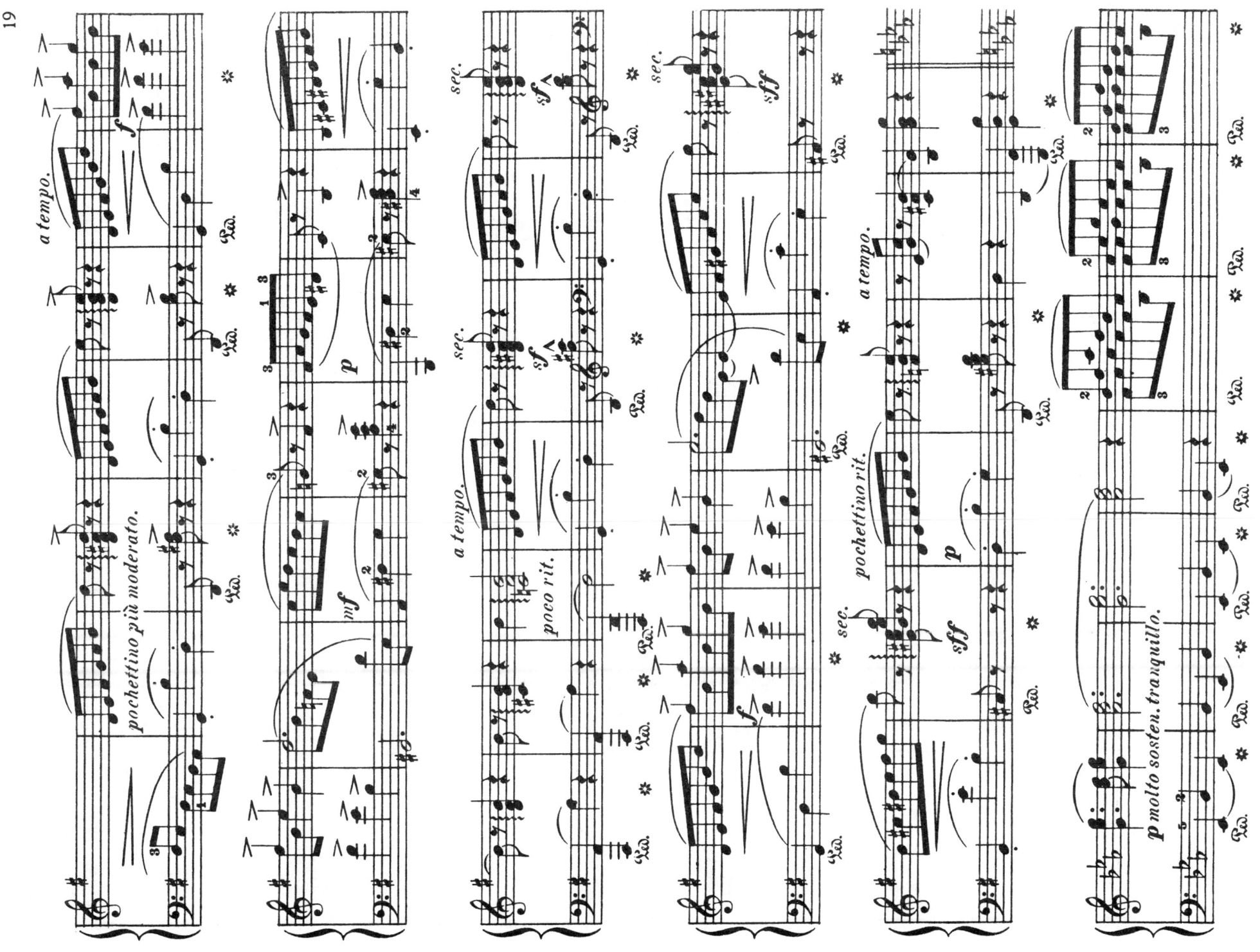

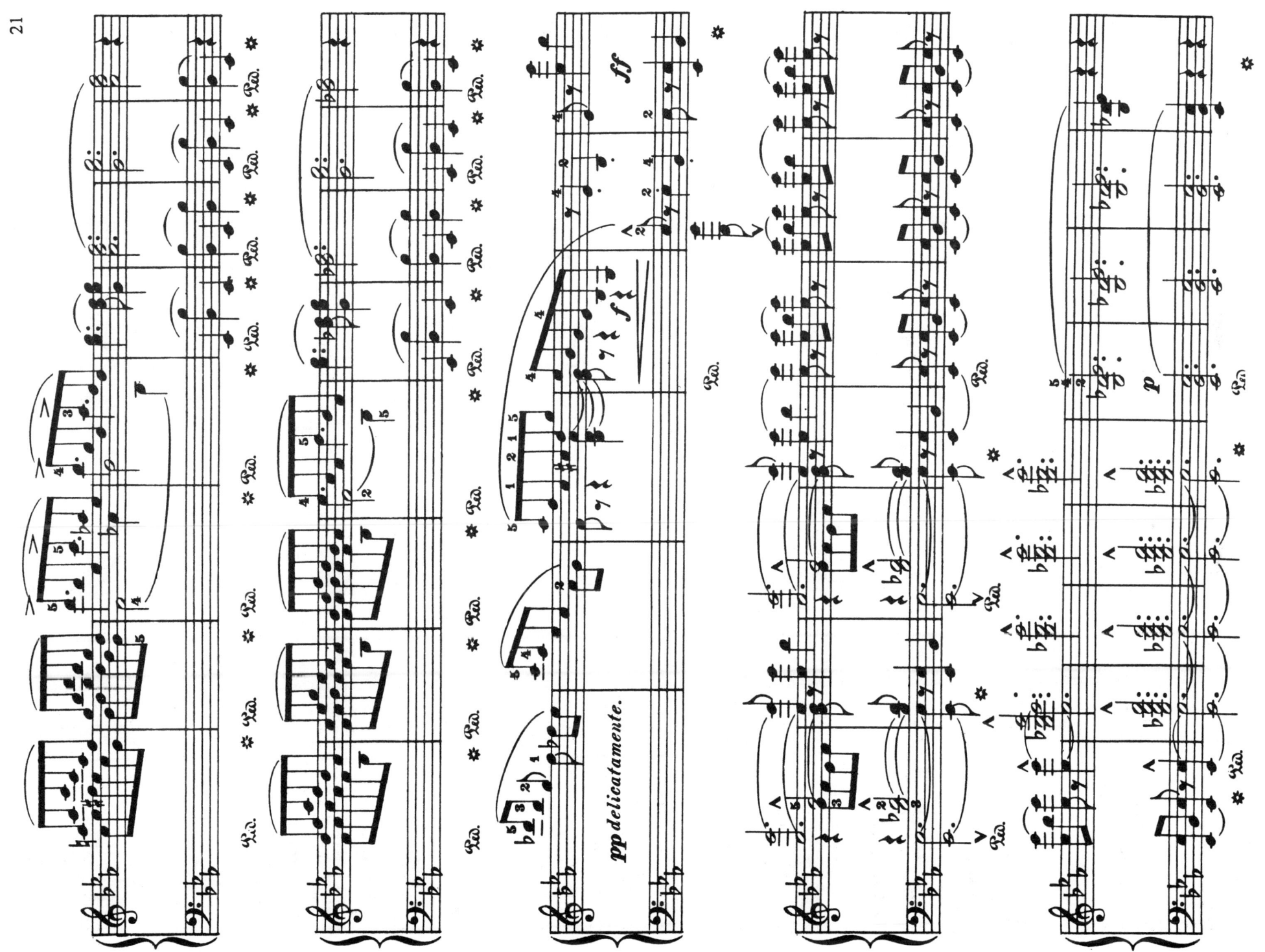

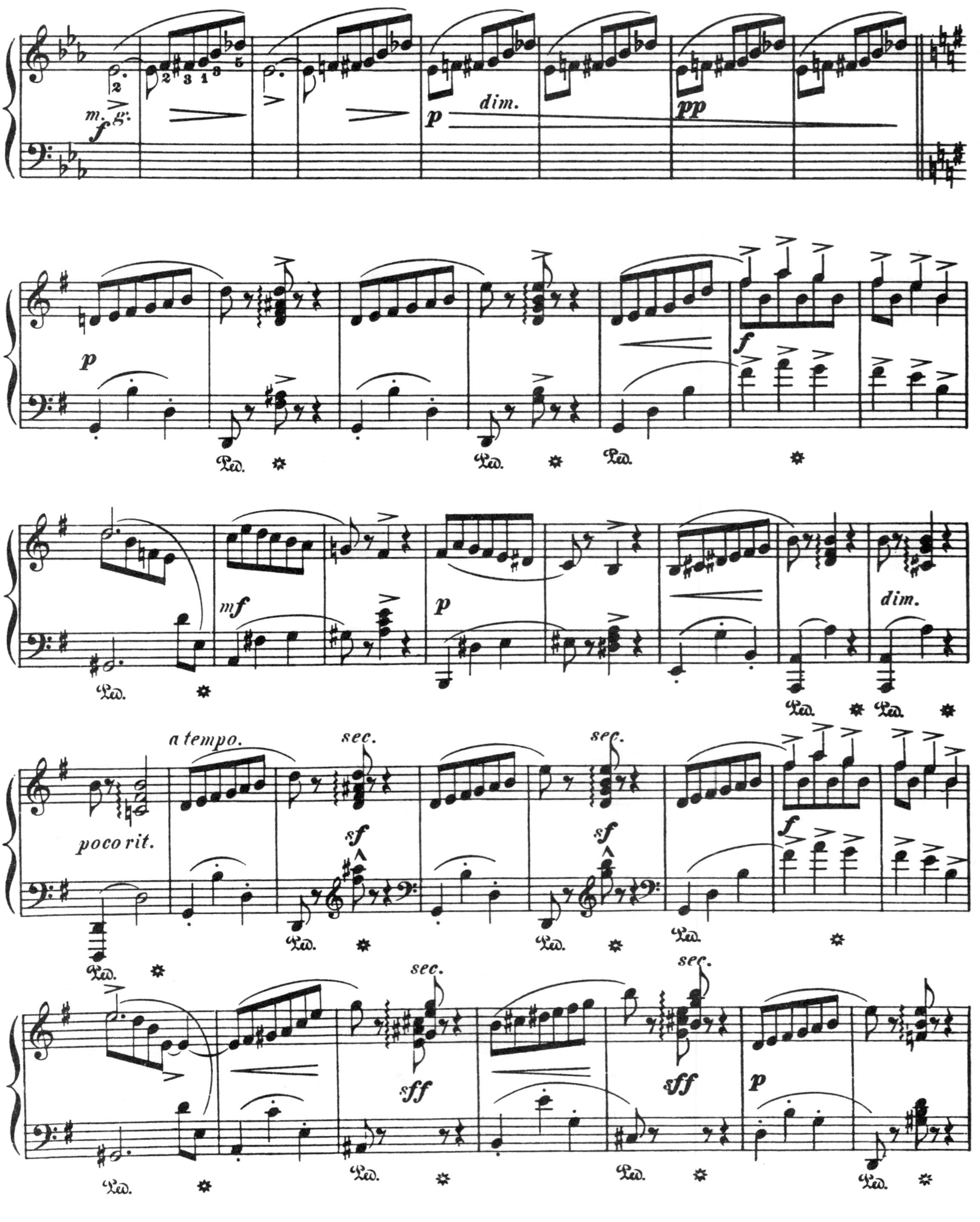

22

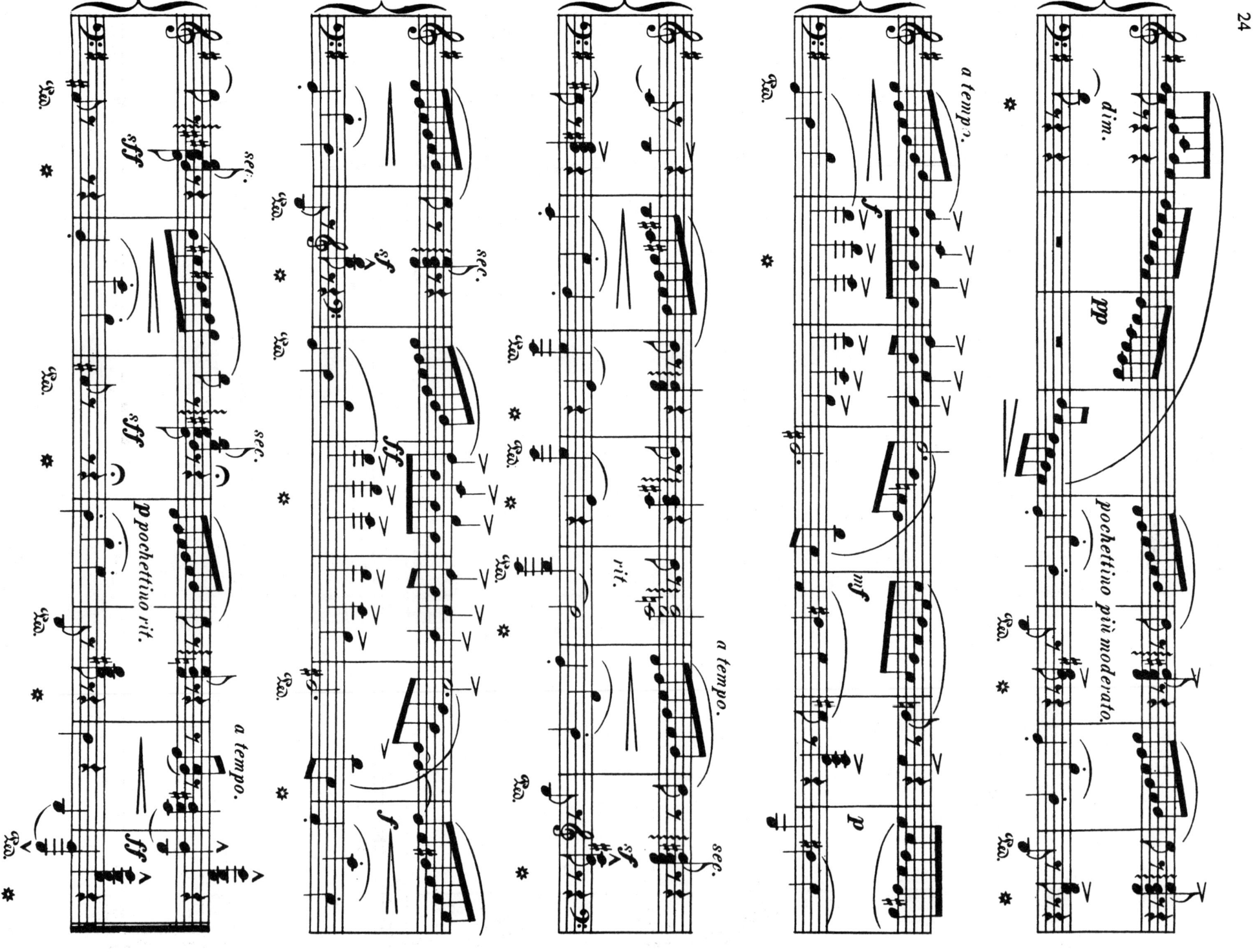

PAS DES AMPHORES
Air de Ballet
Opus 37, No. 2

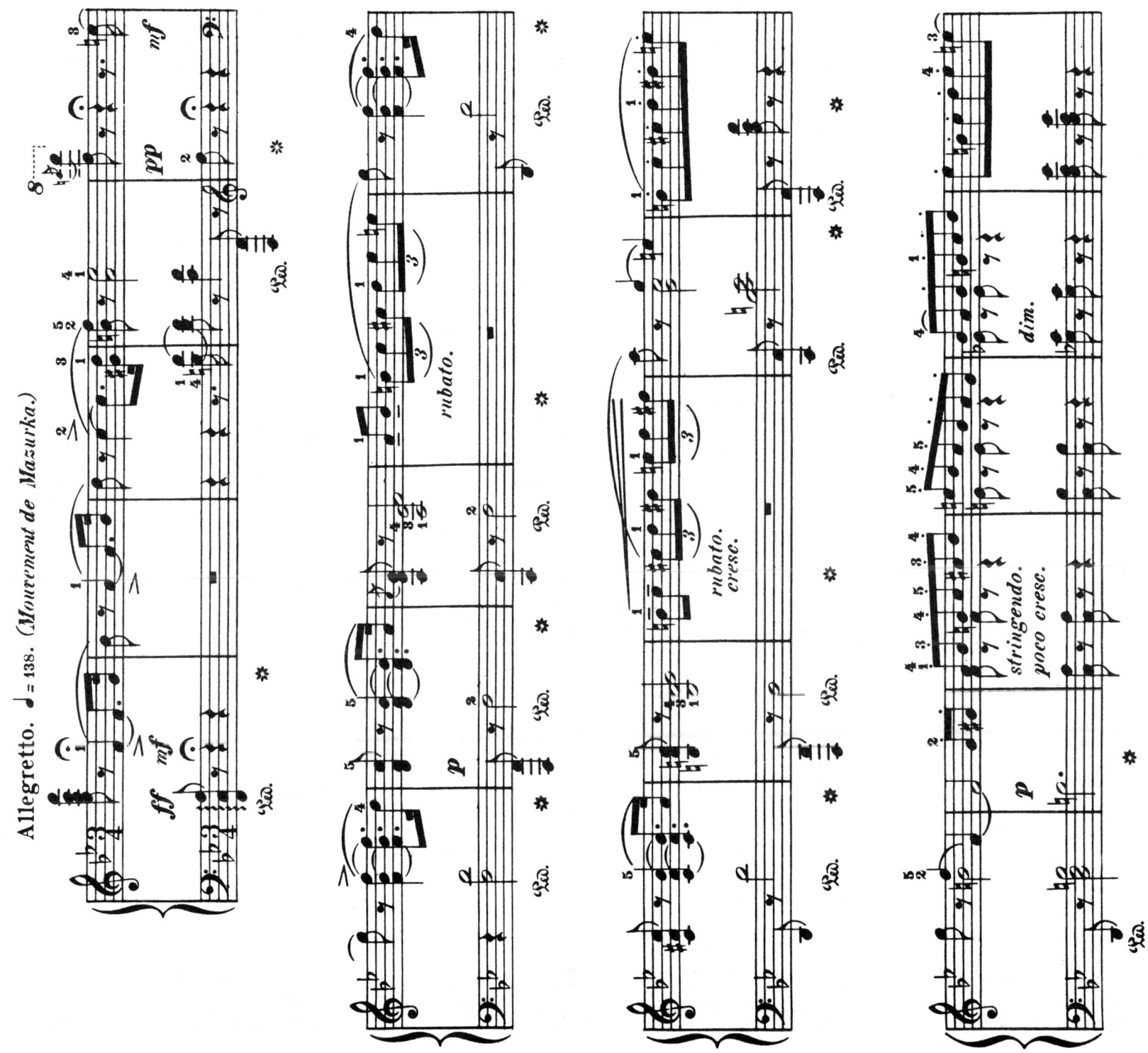

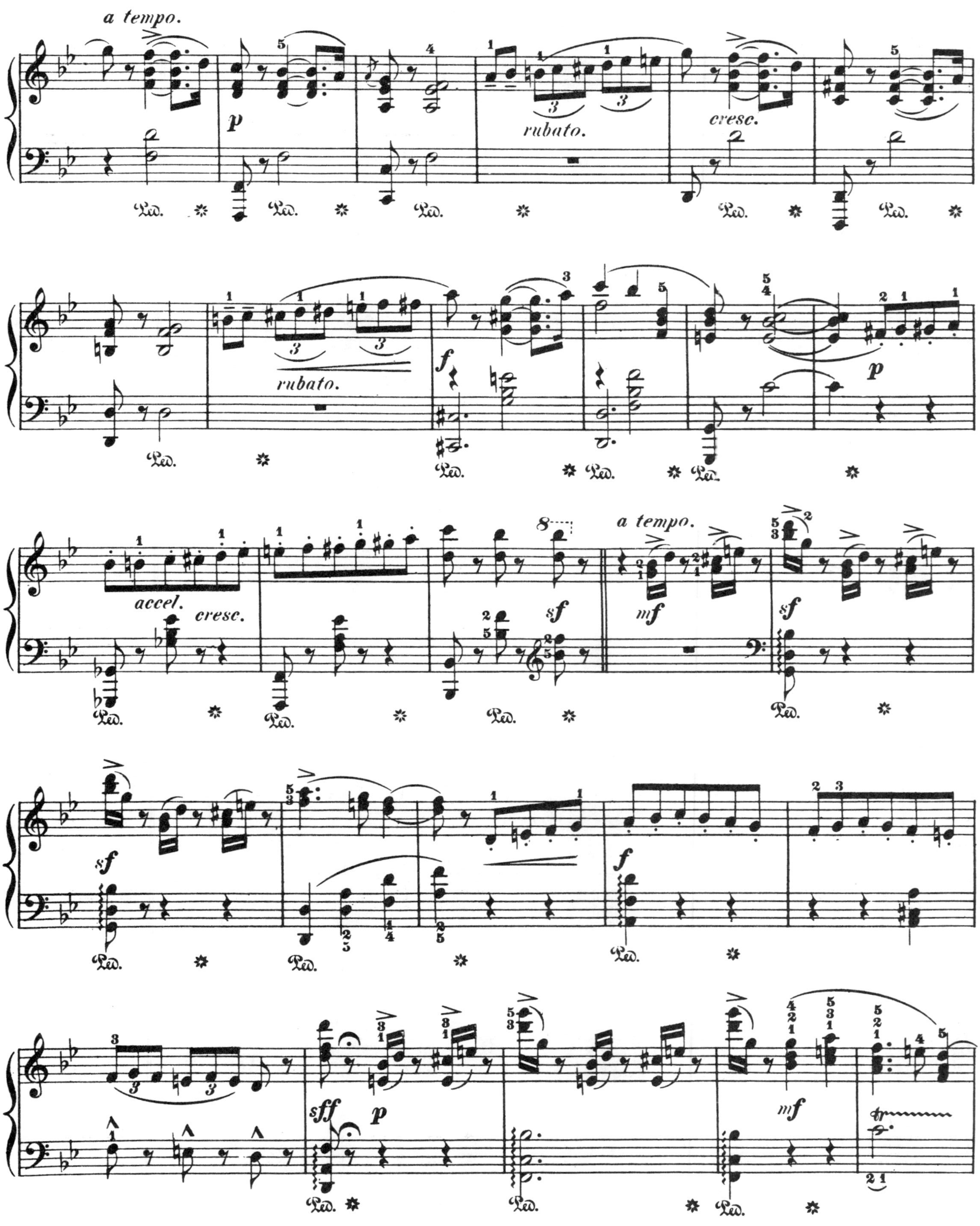
a tempo.
p
rubato.
cresc.
rubato.
f
p
accel.
cresc.
sf
a tempo.
mf
sf
sf
f
sff
p
mf

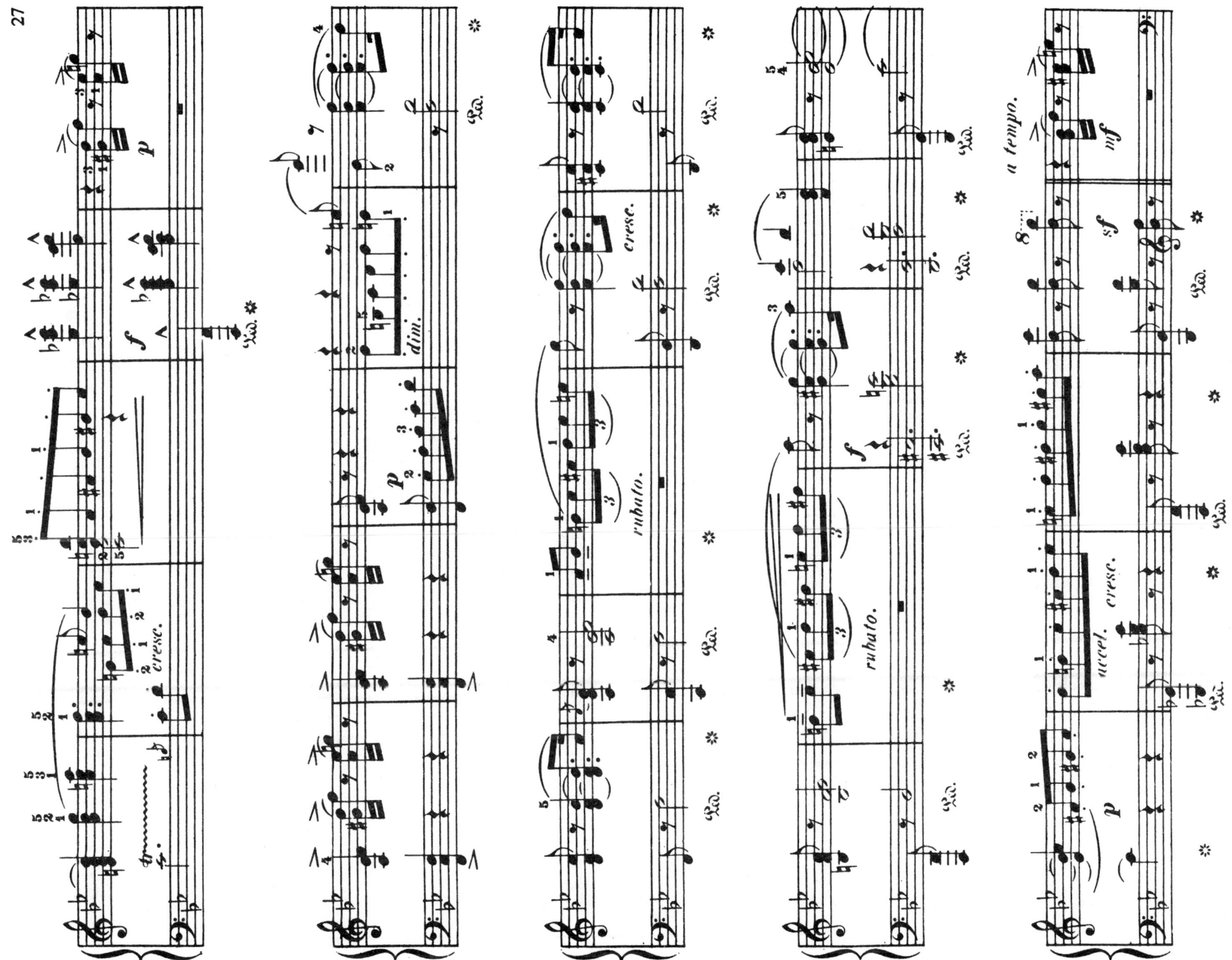

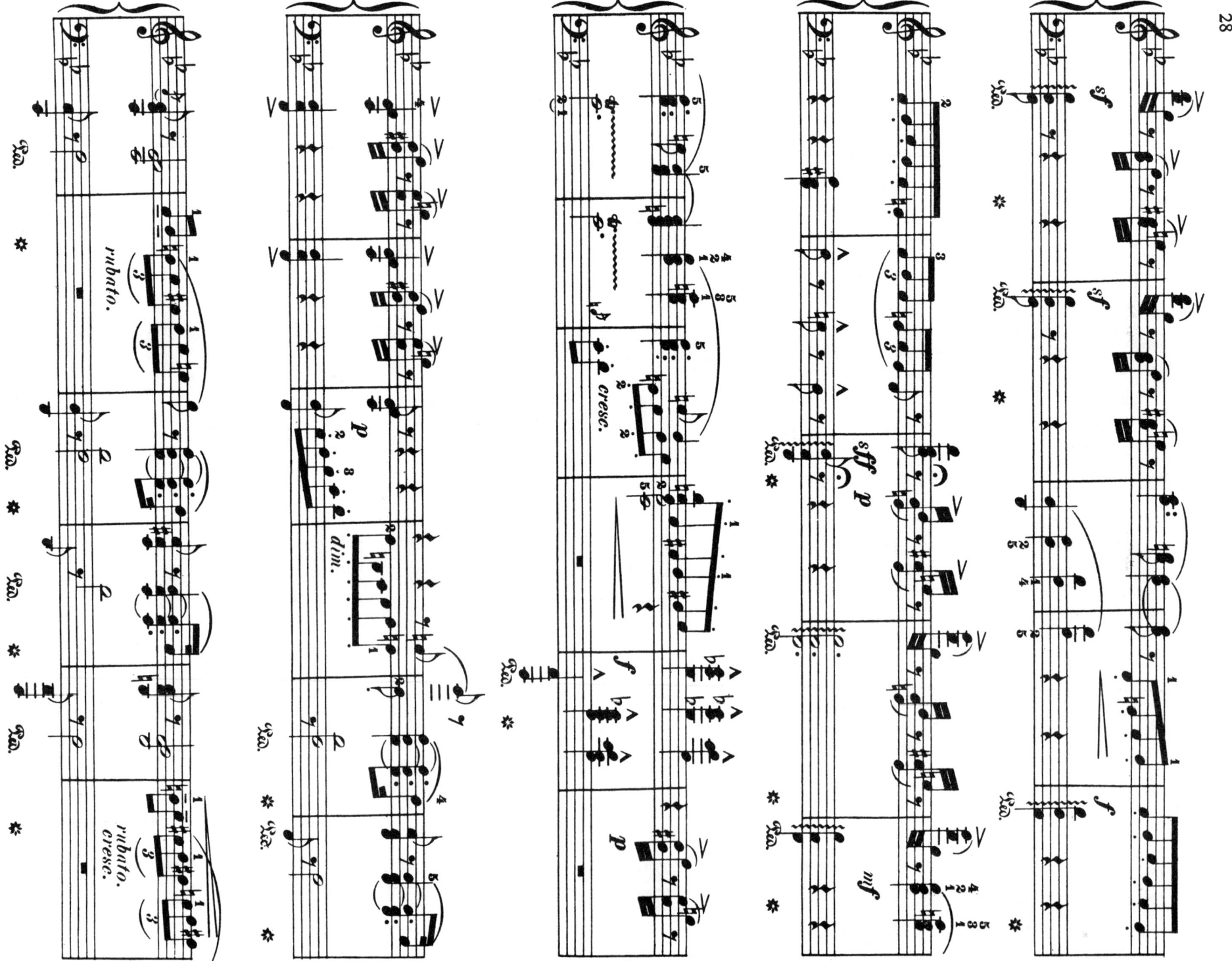

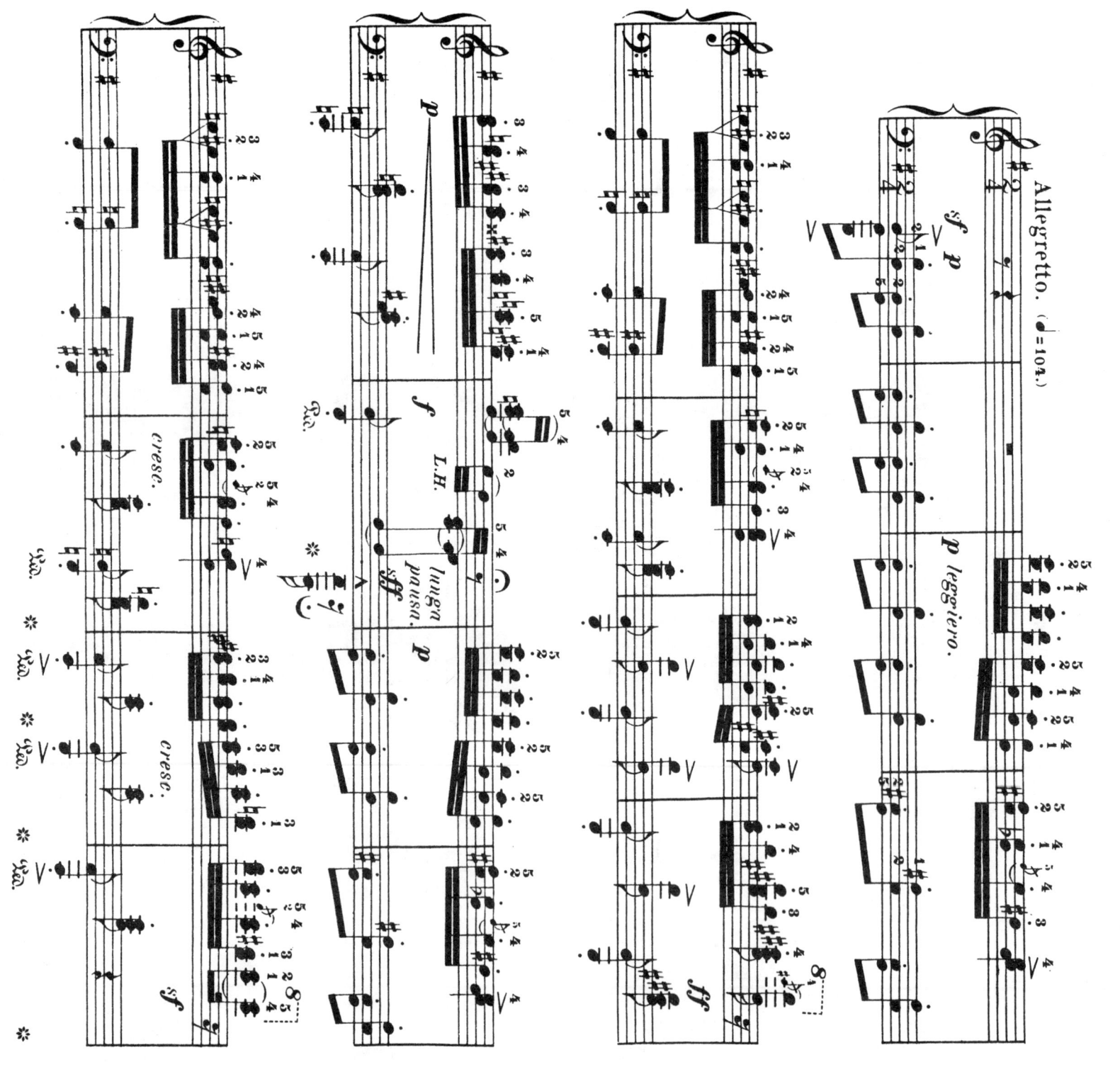

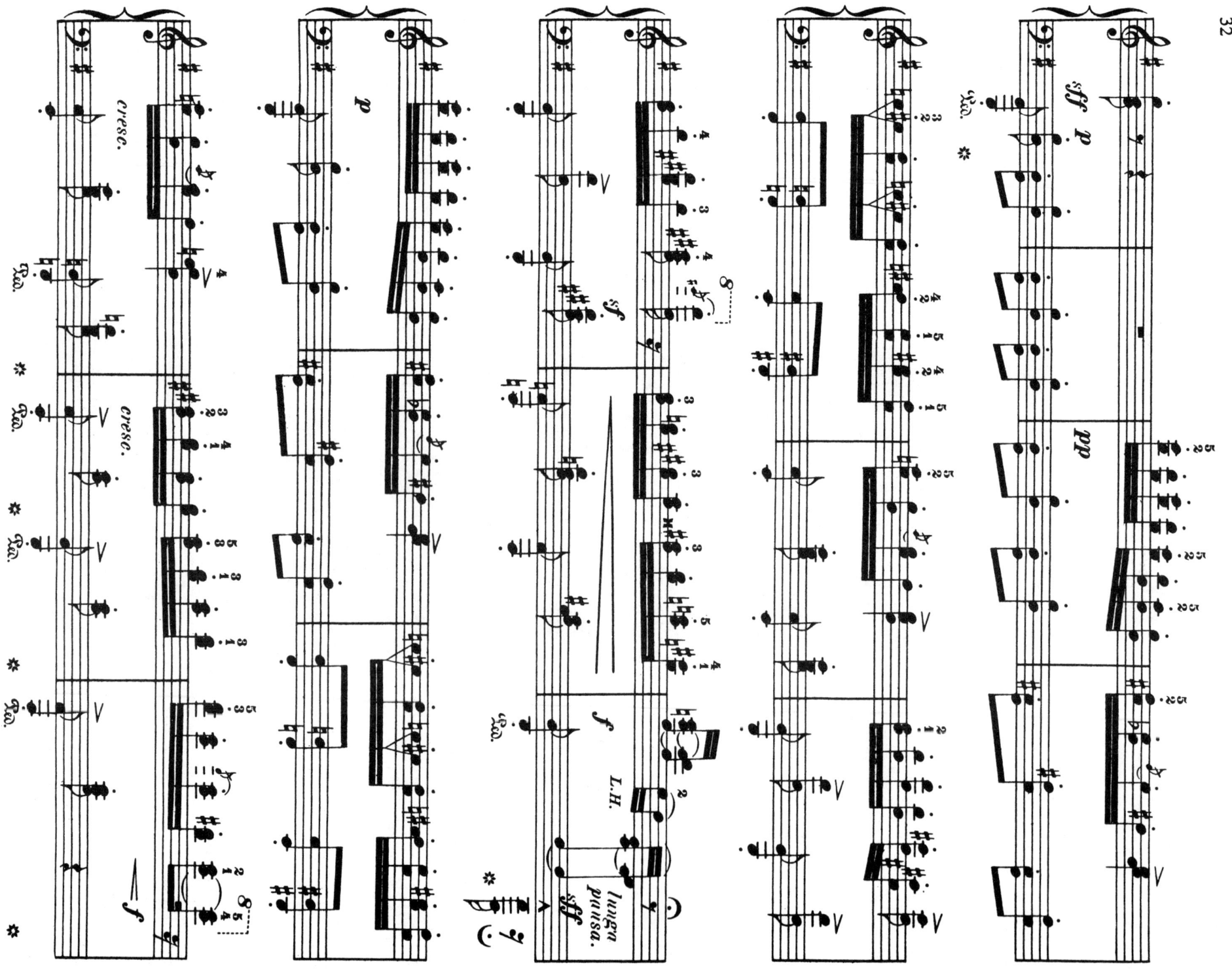

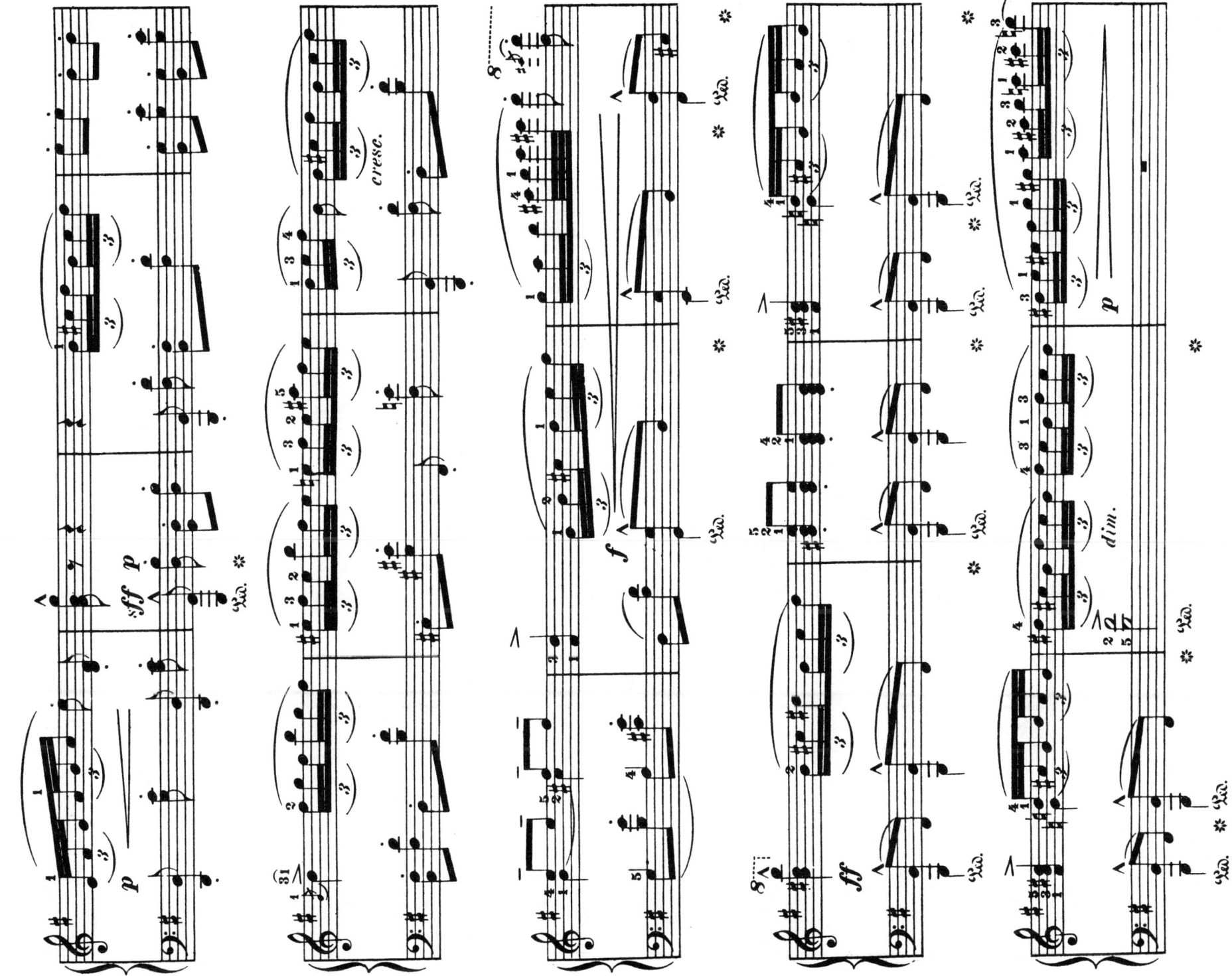

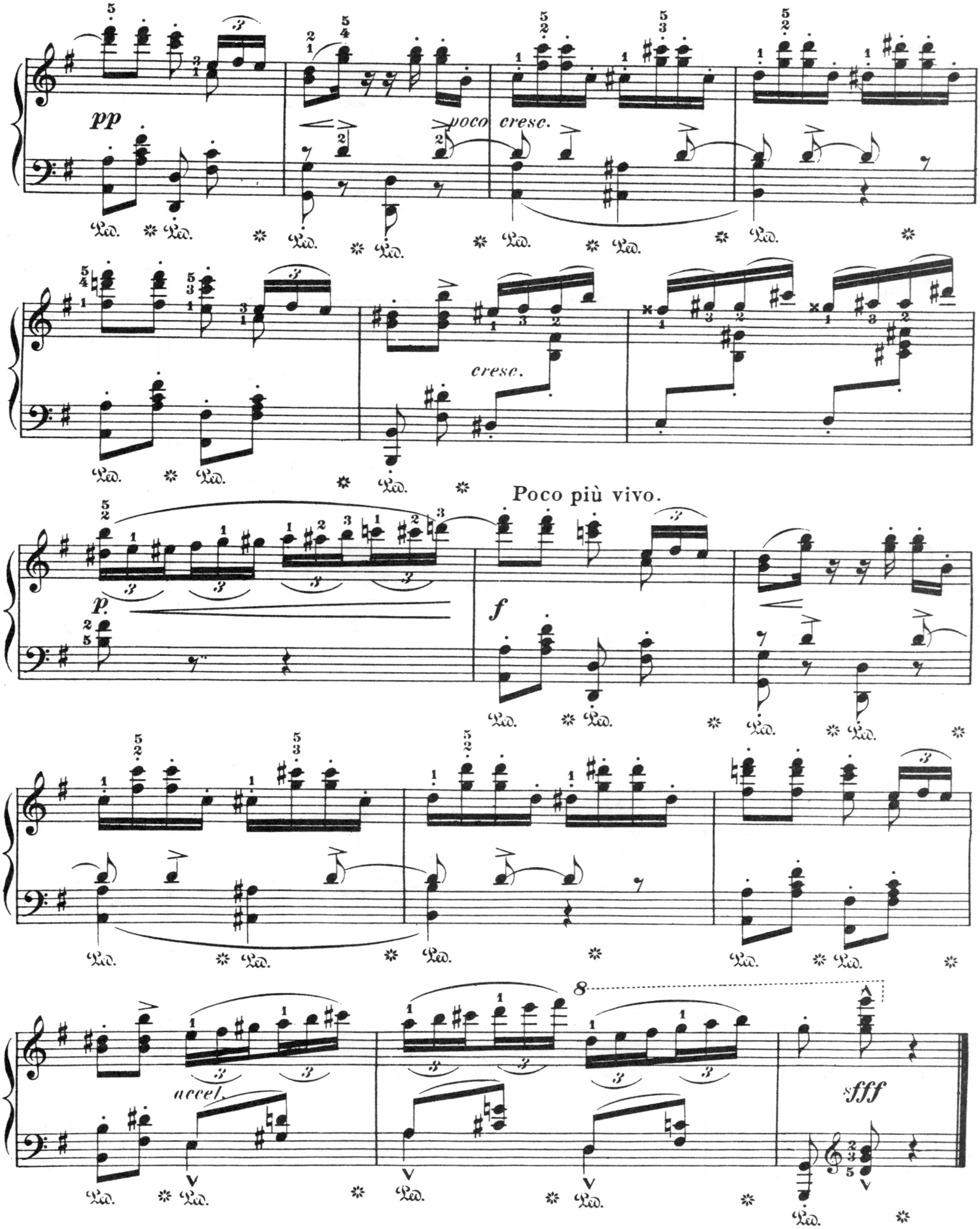
pp
poco cresc.
cresc.
Poco più vivo.
p.
f
accel.
8
sfff

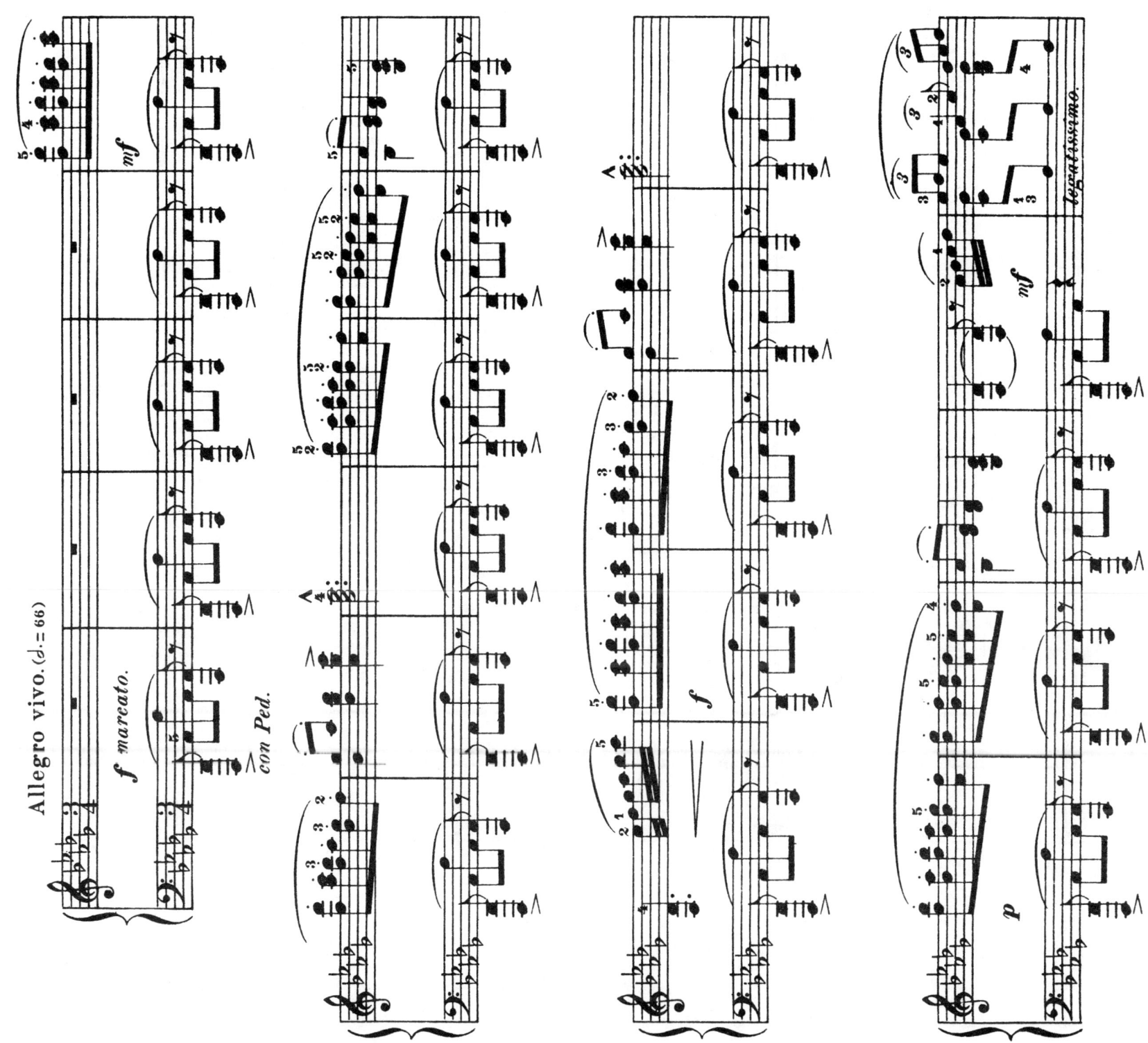

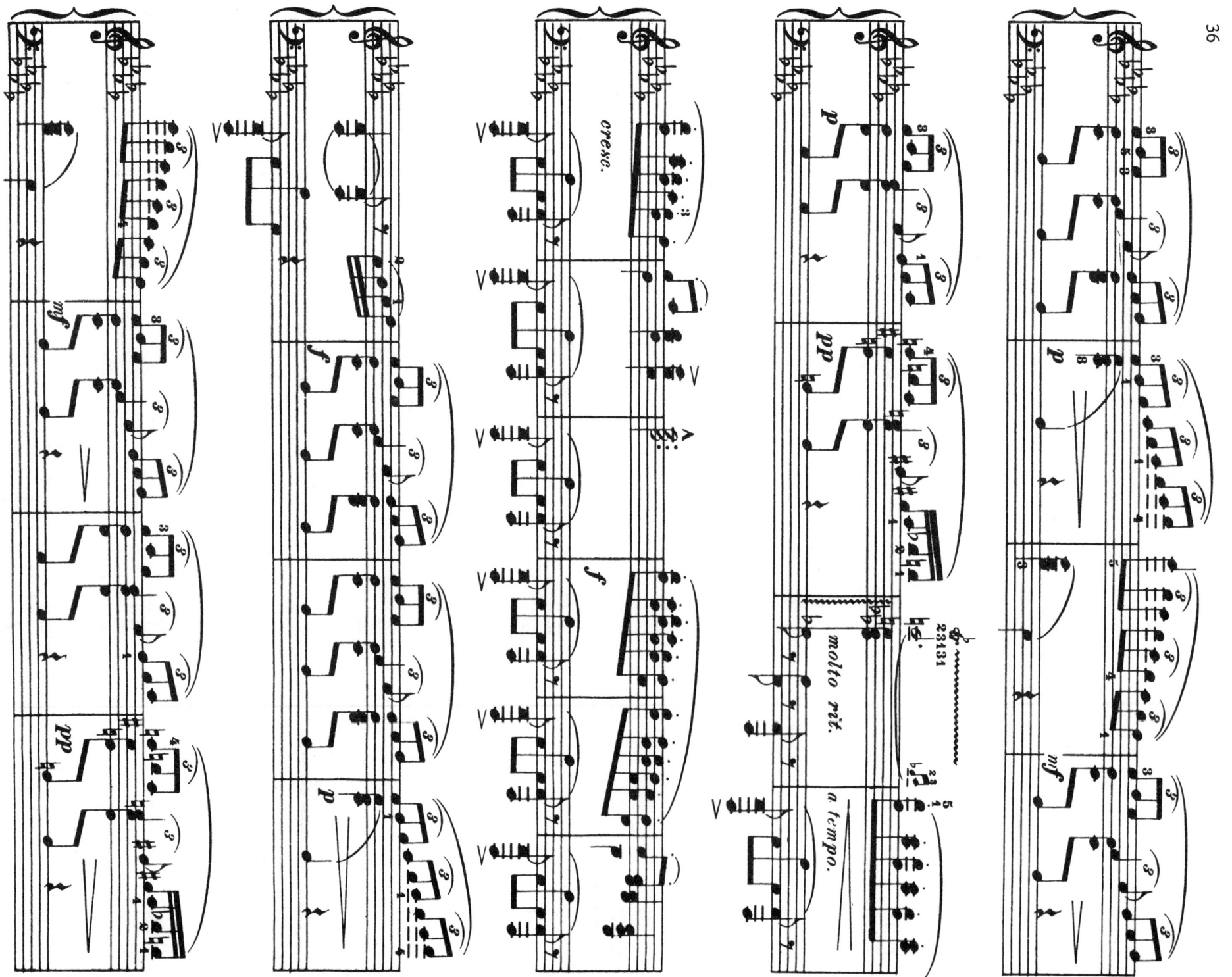

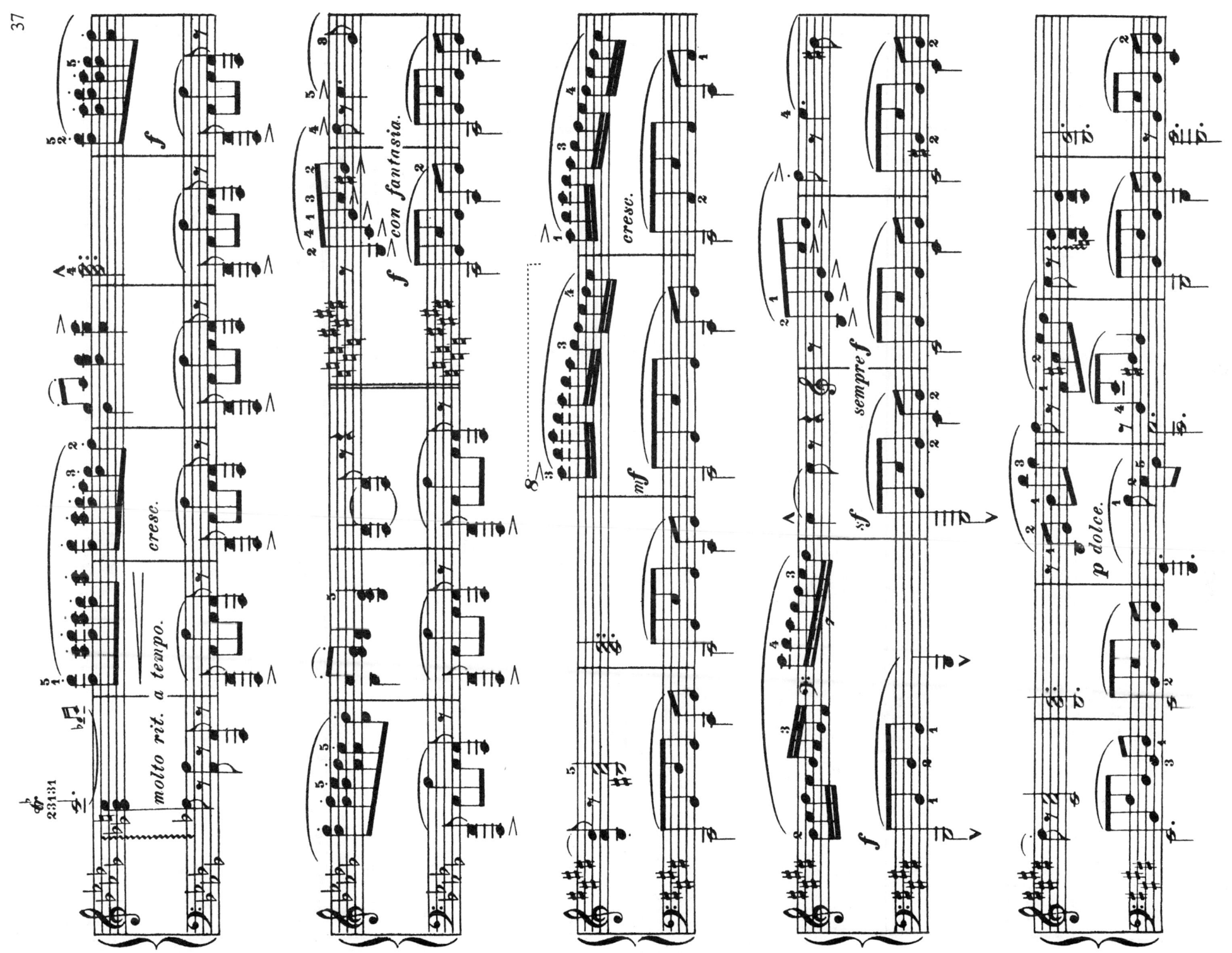

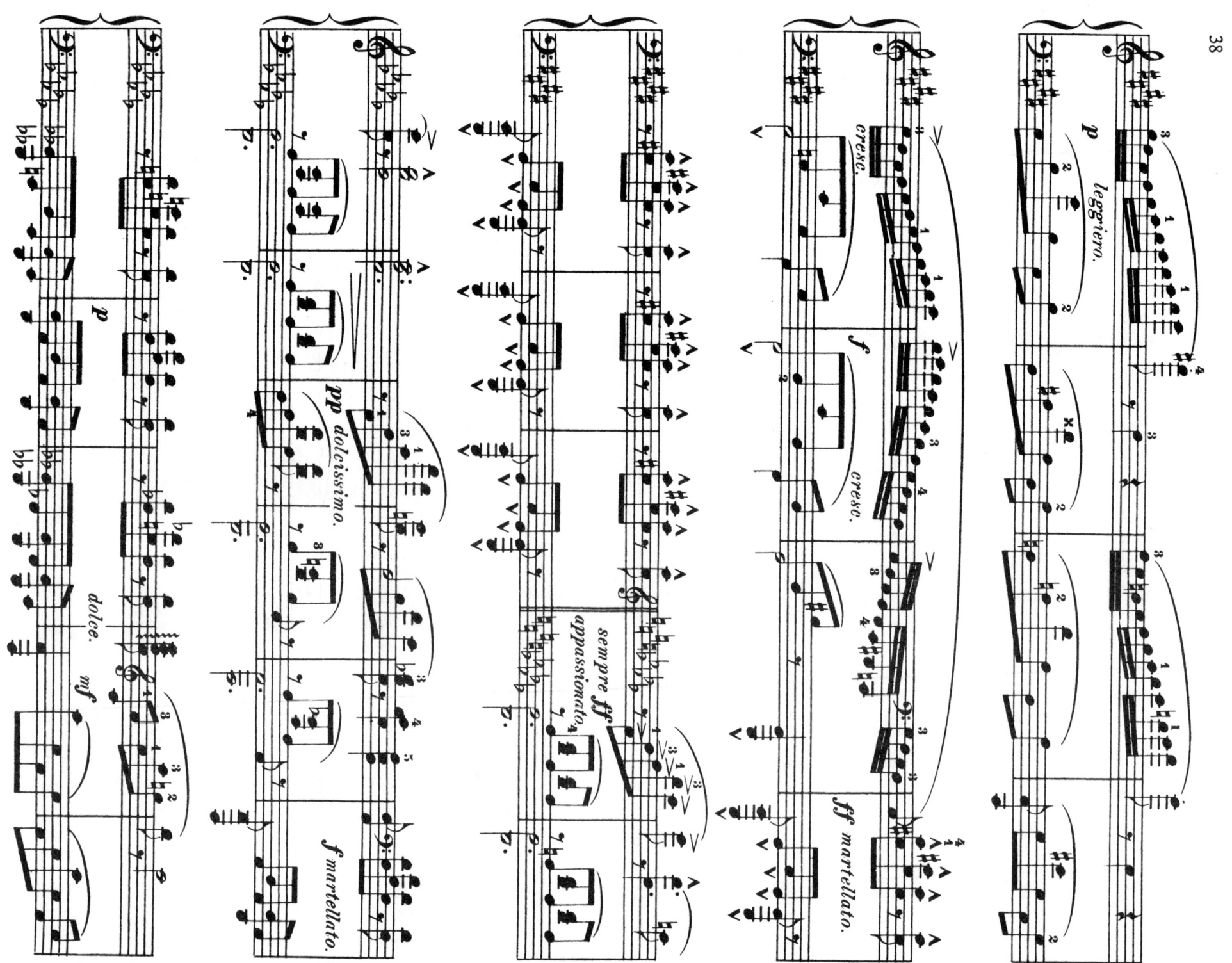

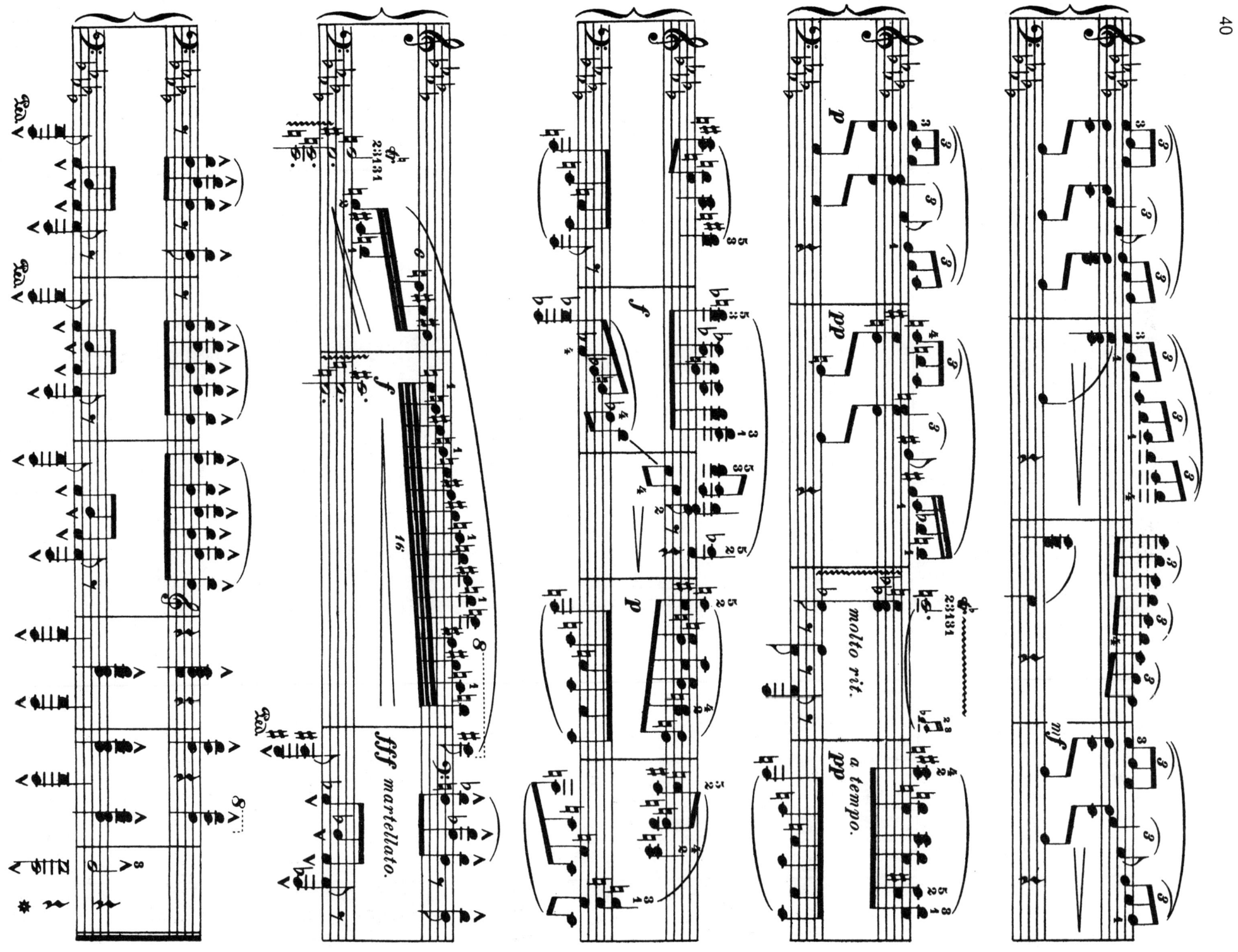

SCARF-DANCE
Scène de Ballet
Opus 37, No. 3

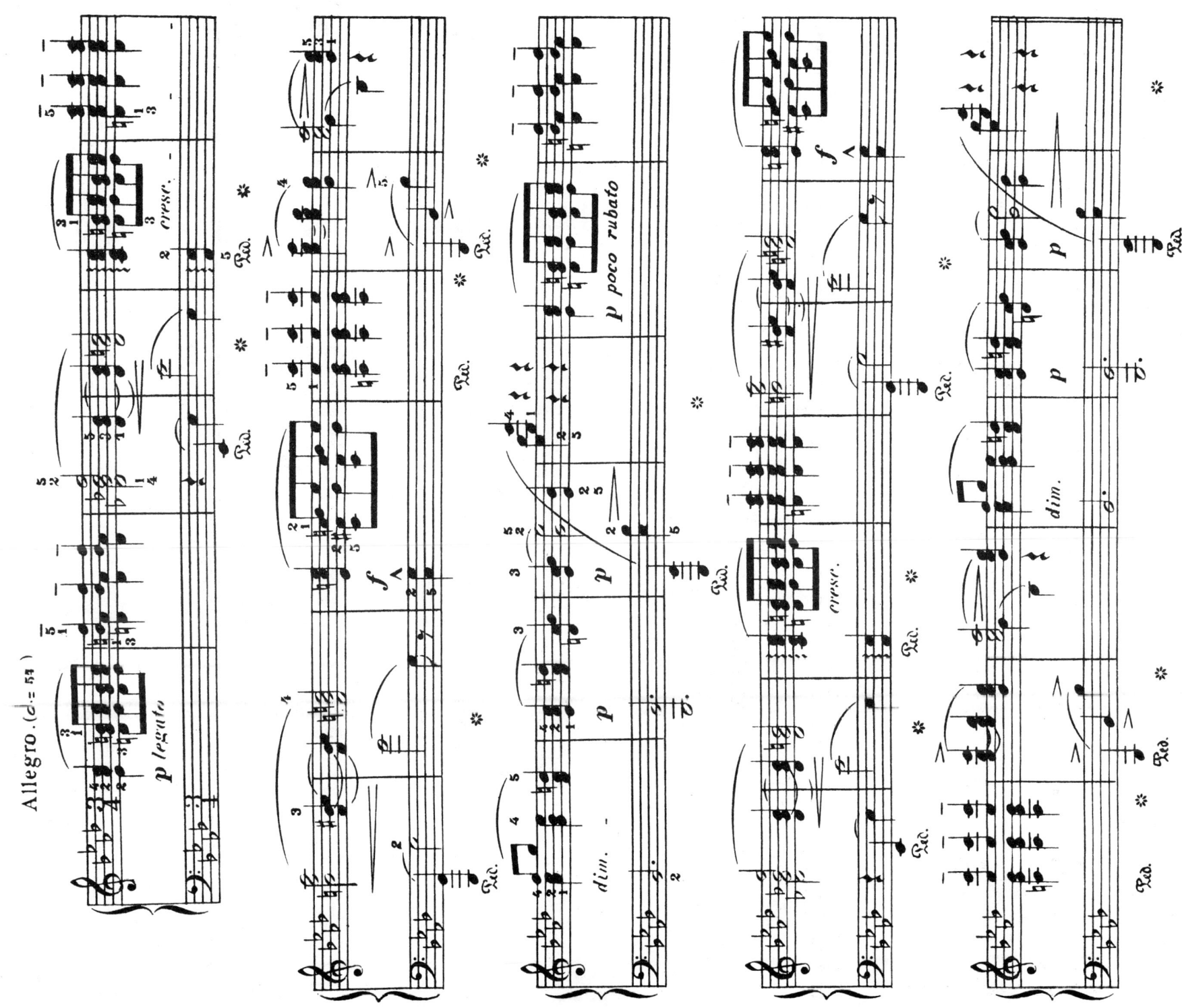

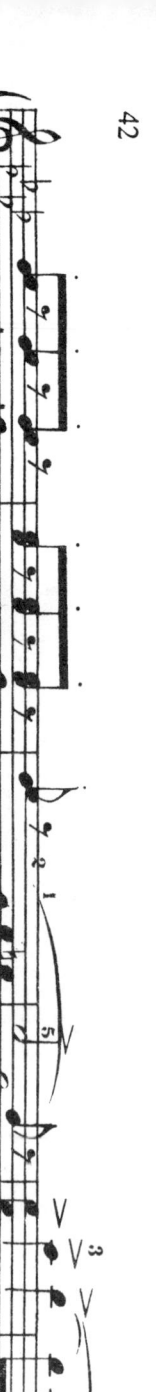

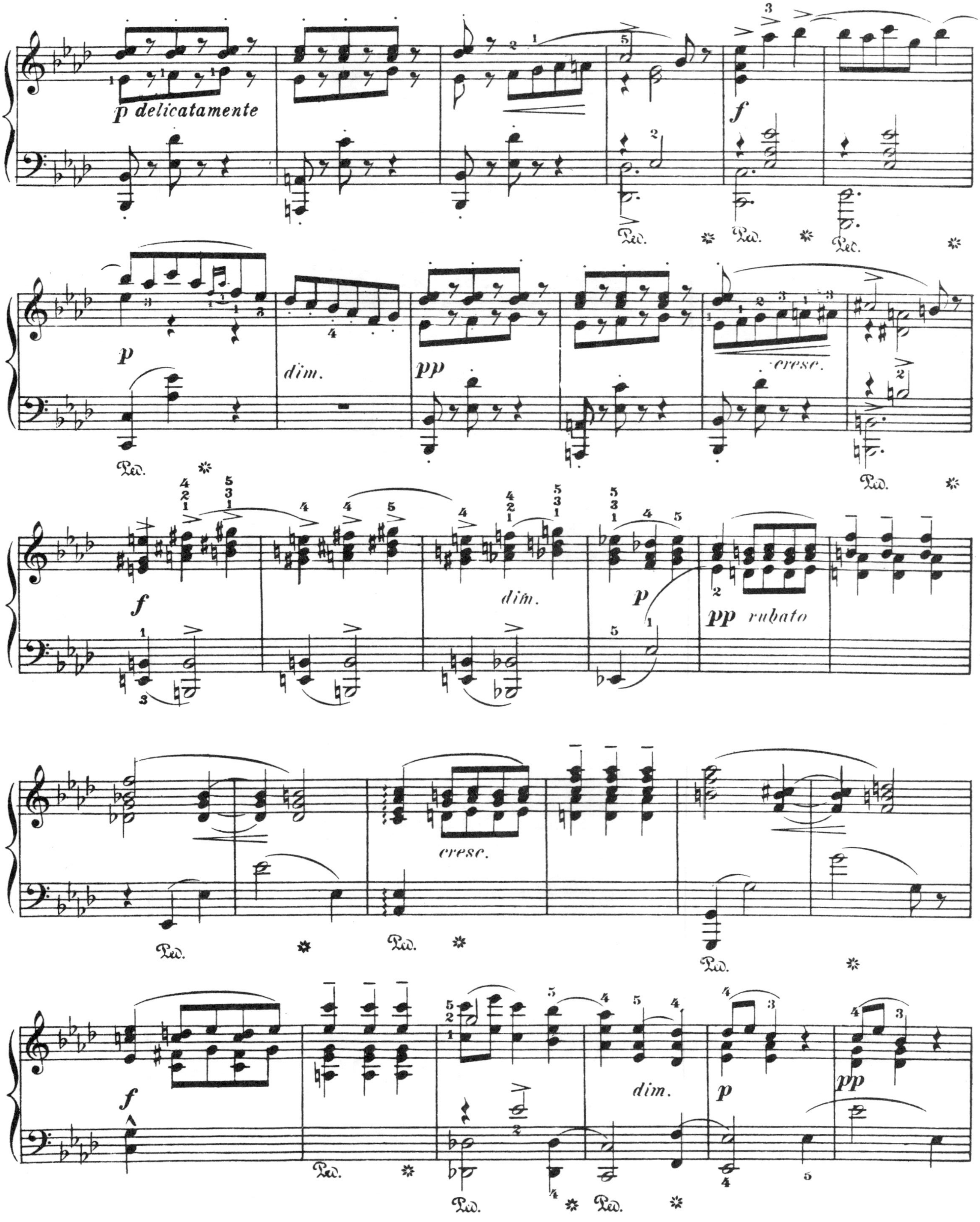
p delicatamente
f
p
dim.
pp
cresc.
f
dim.
p
pp rubato
cresc.
f
dim.
p
pp

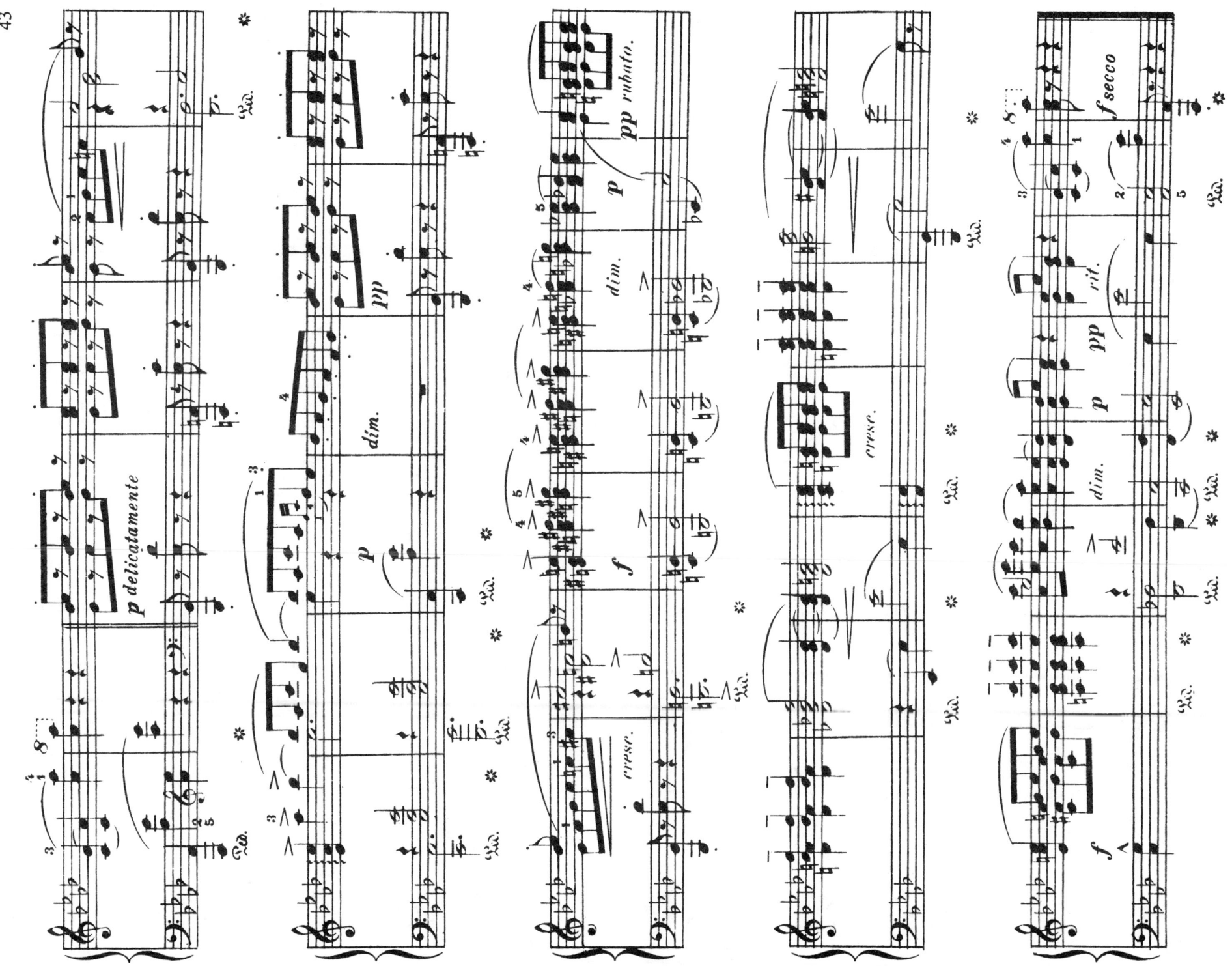

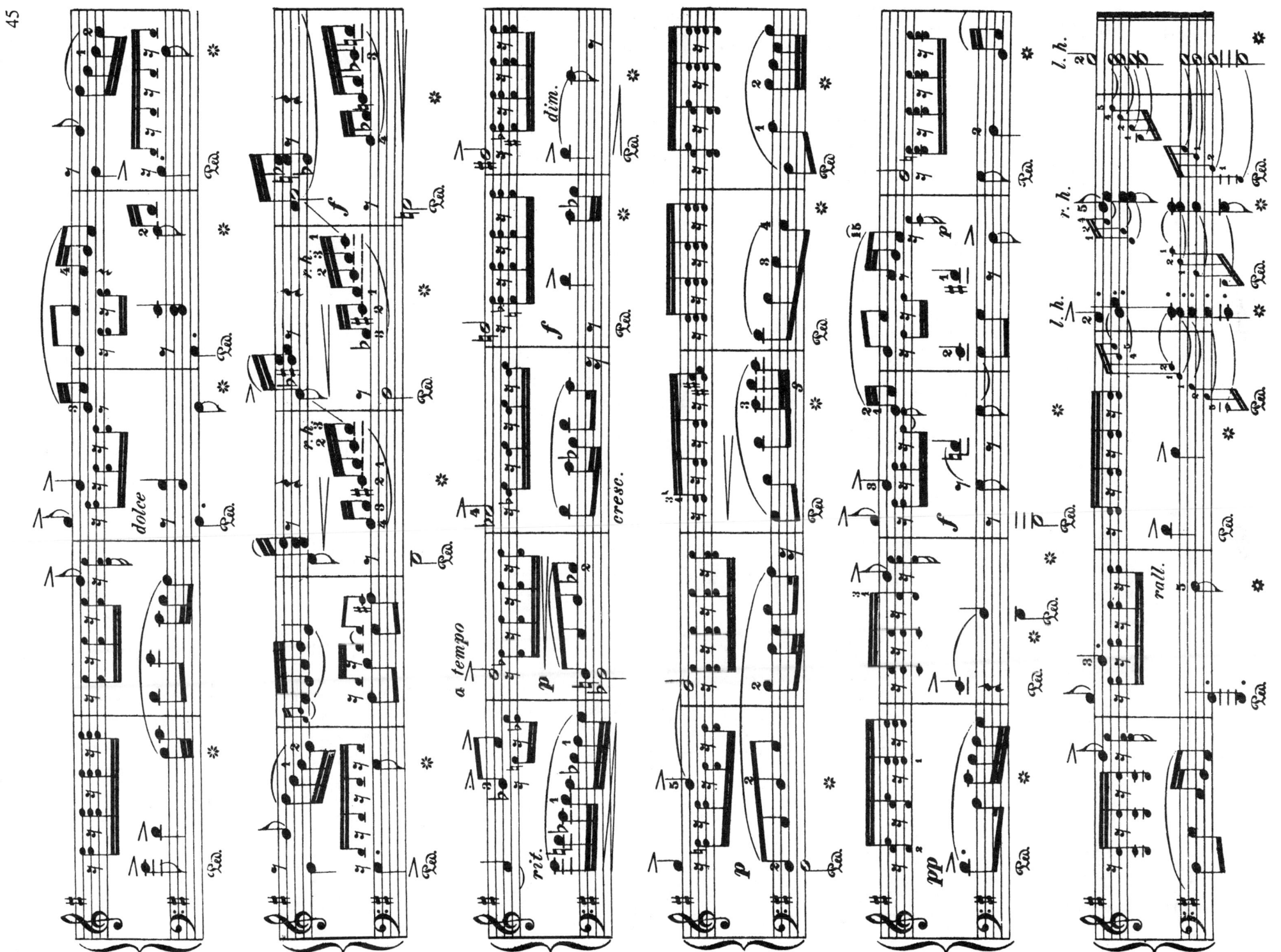

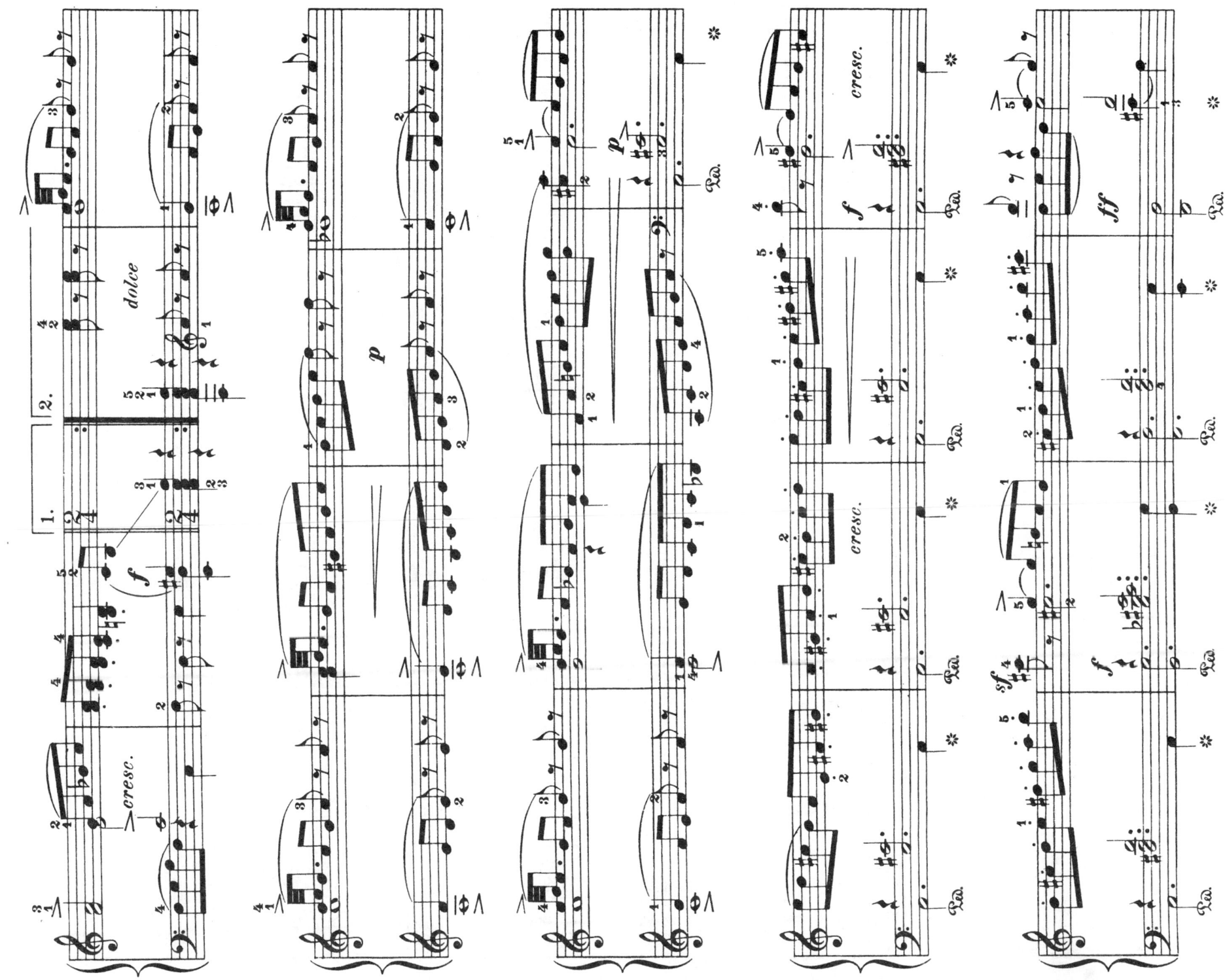

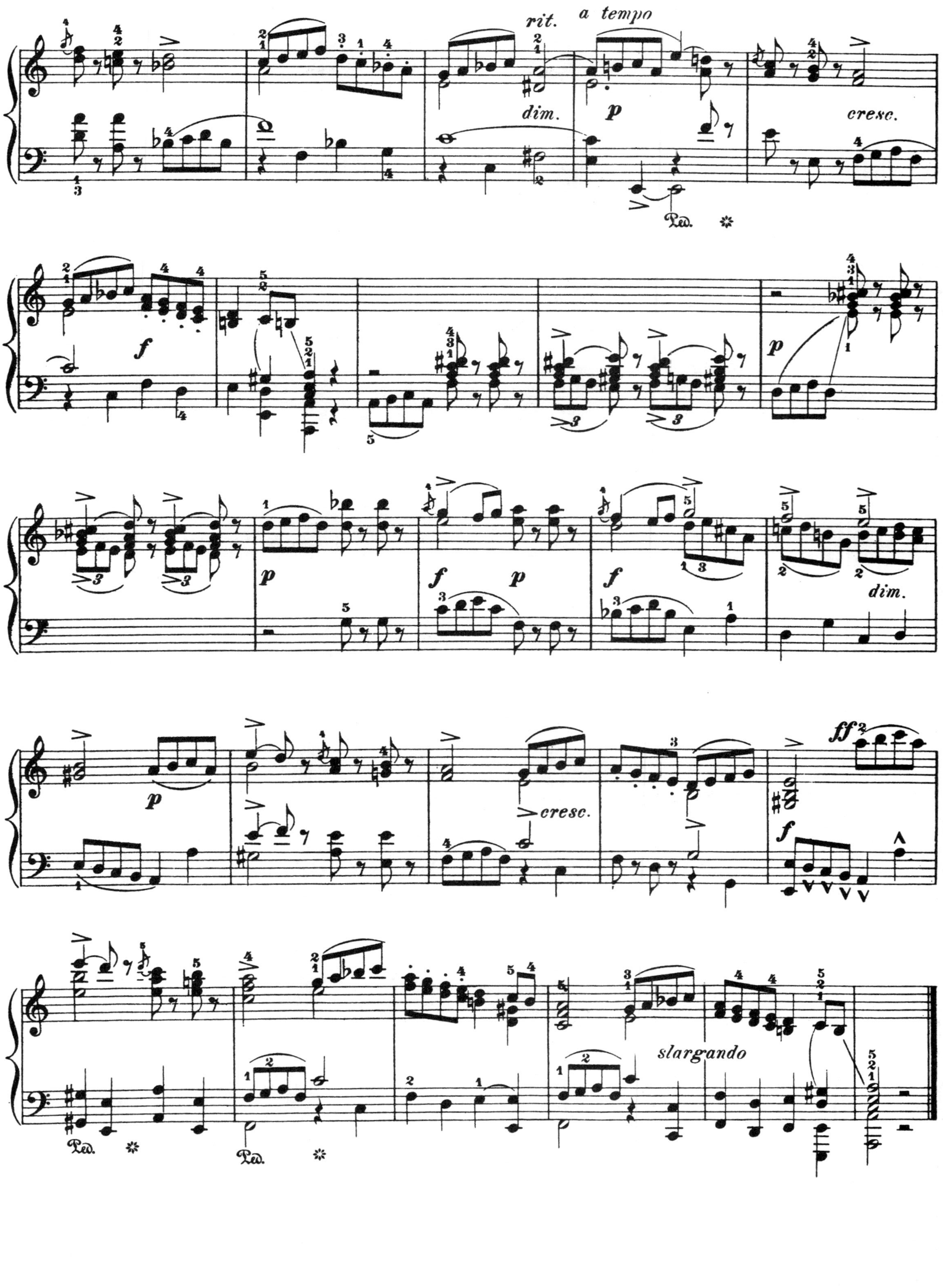
rit.
a tempo
dim.
p
cresc.
Ped.
f
p
p
f
p
f
dim.
p
cresc.
ff
f
Ped.
Ped.
slargando

PIERRETTE
Air de Ballet
Opus 41

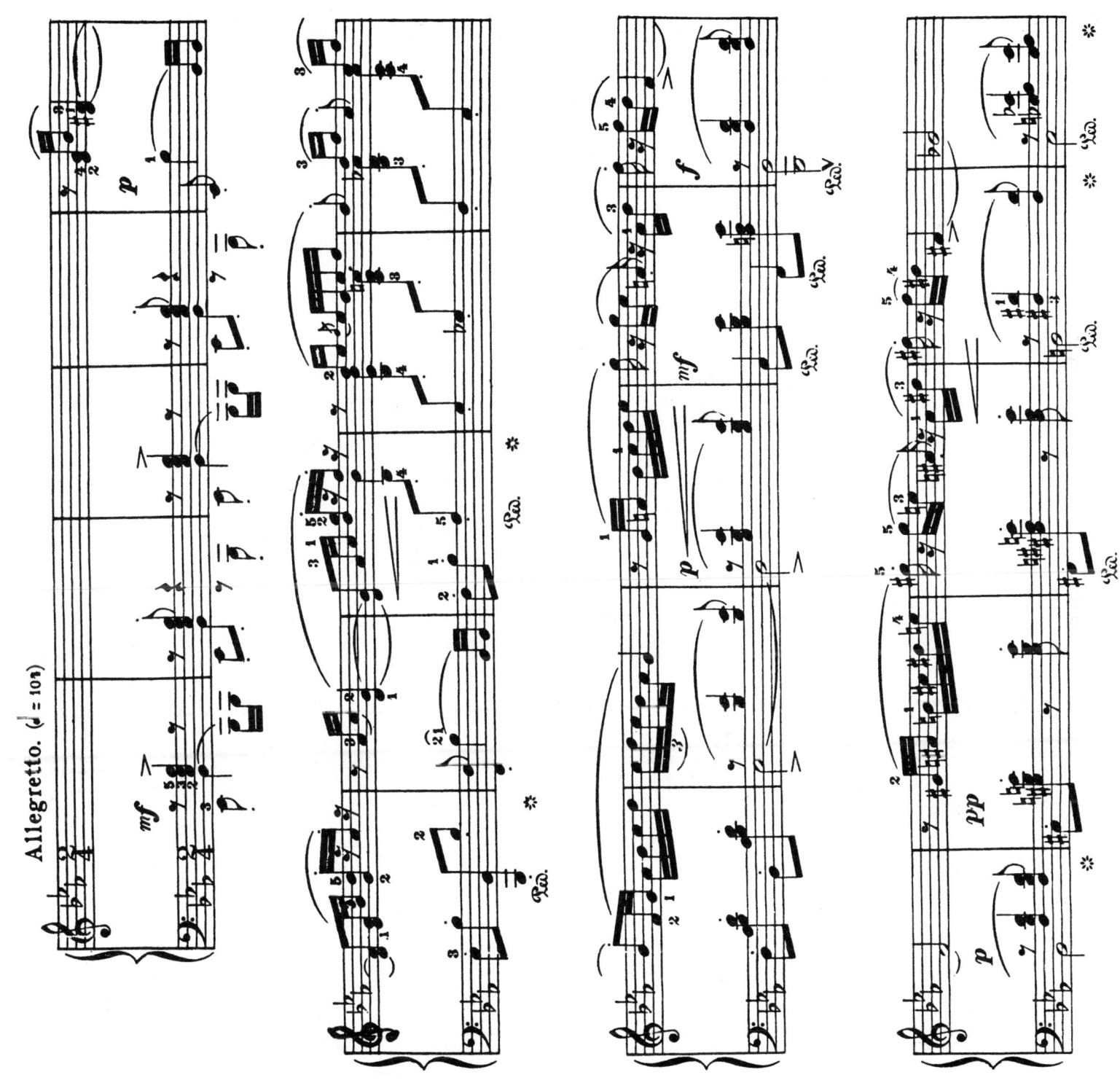

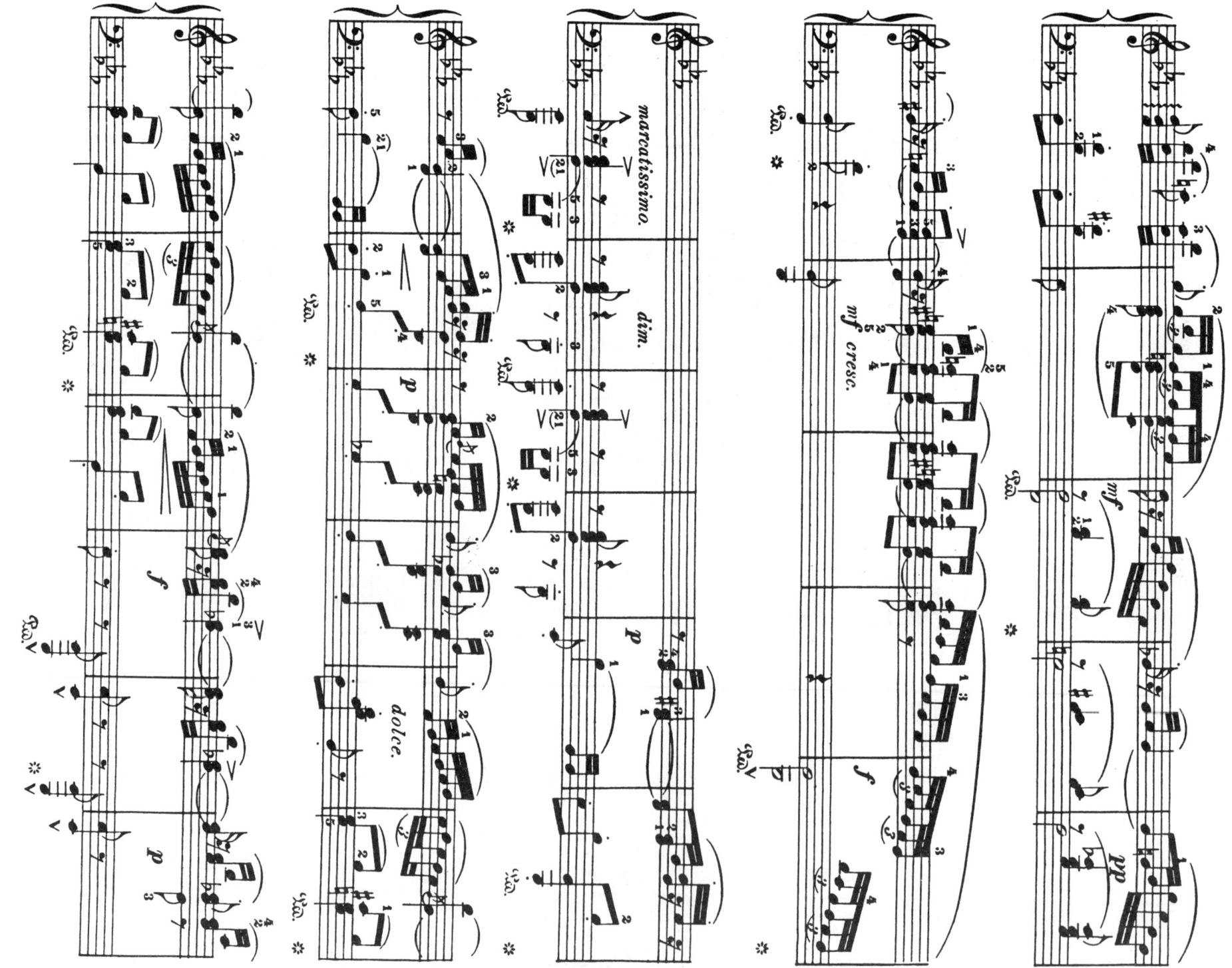

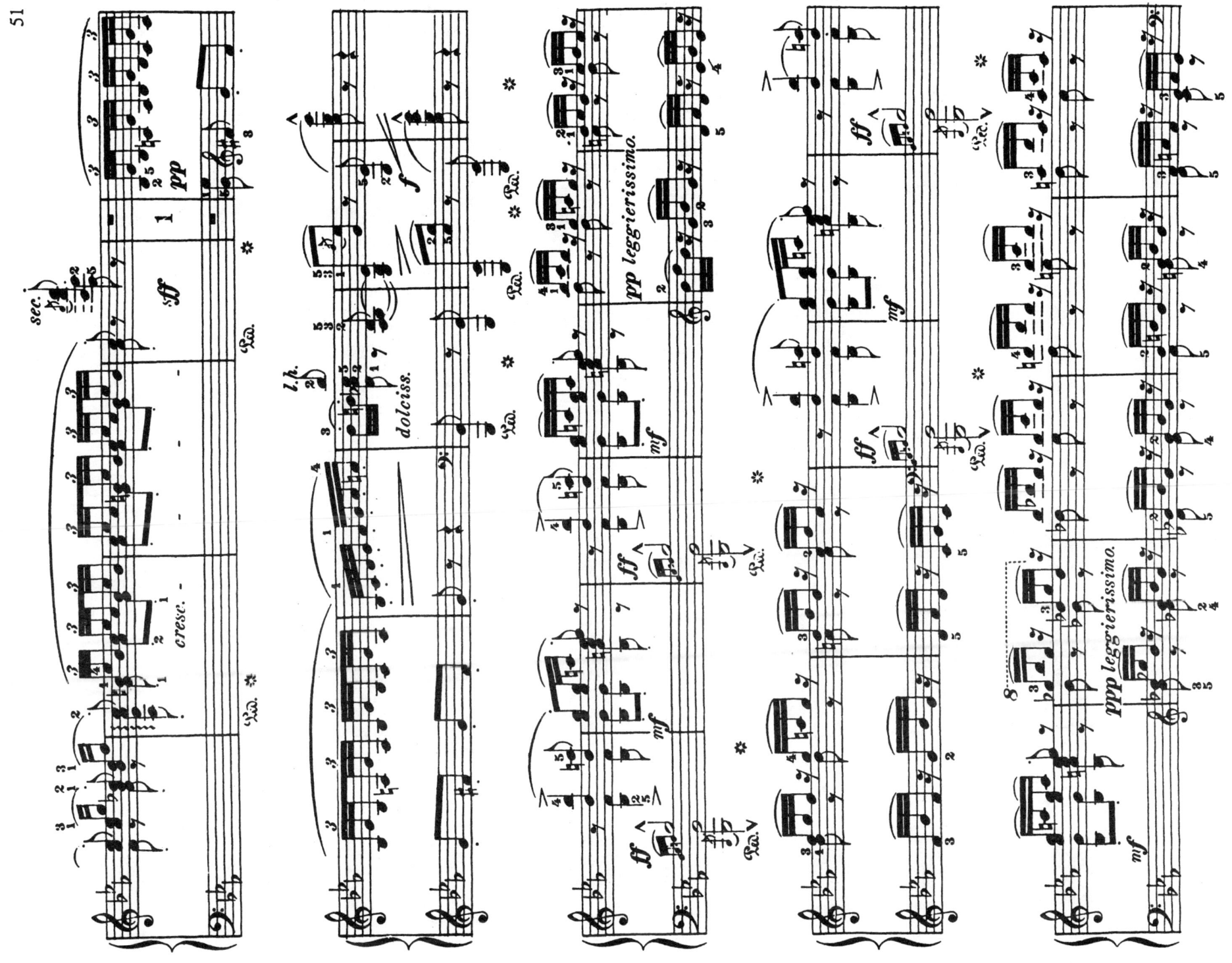

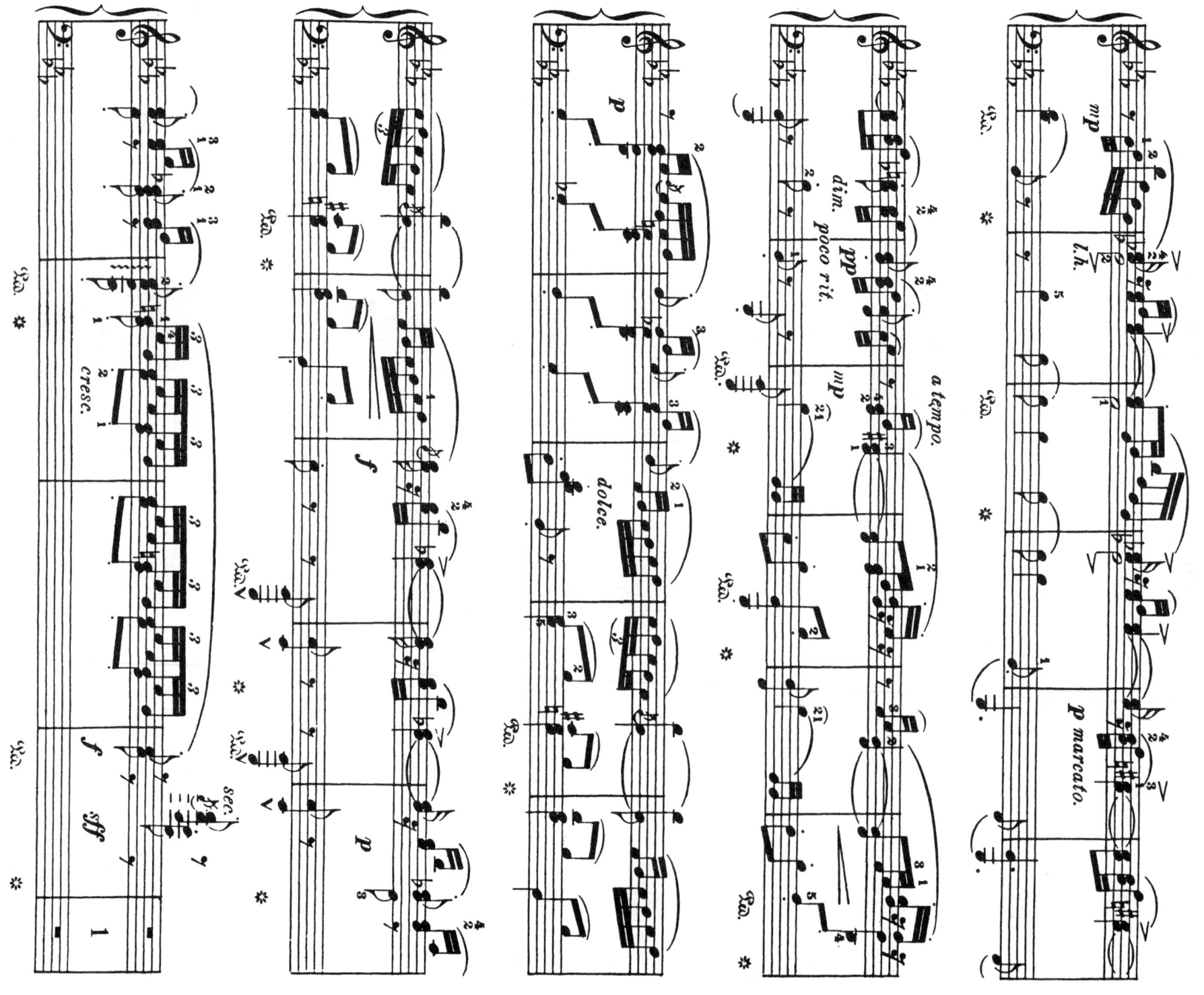

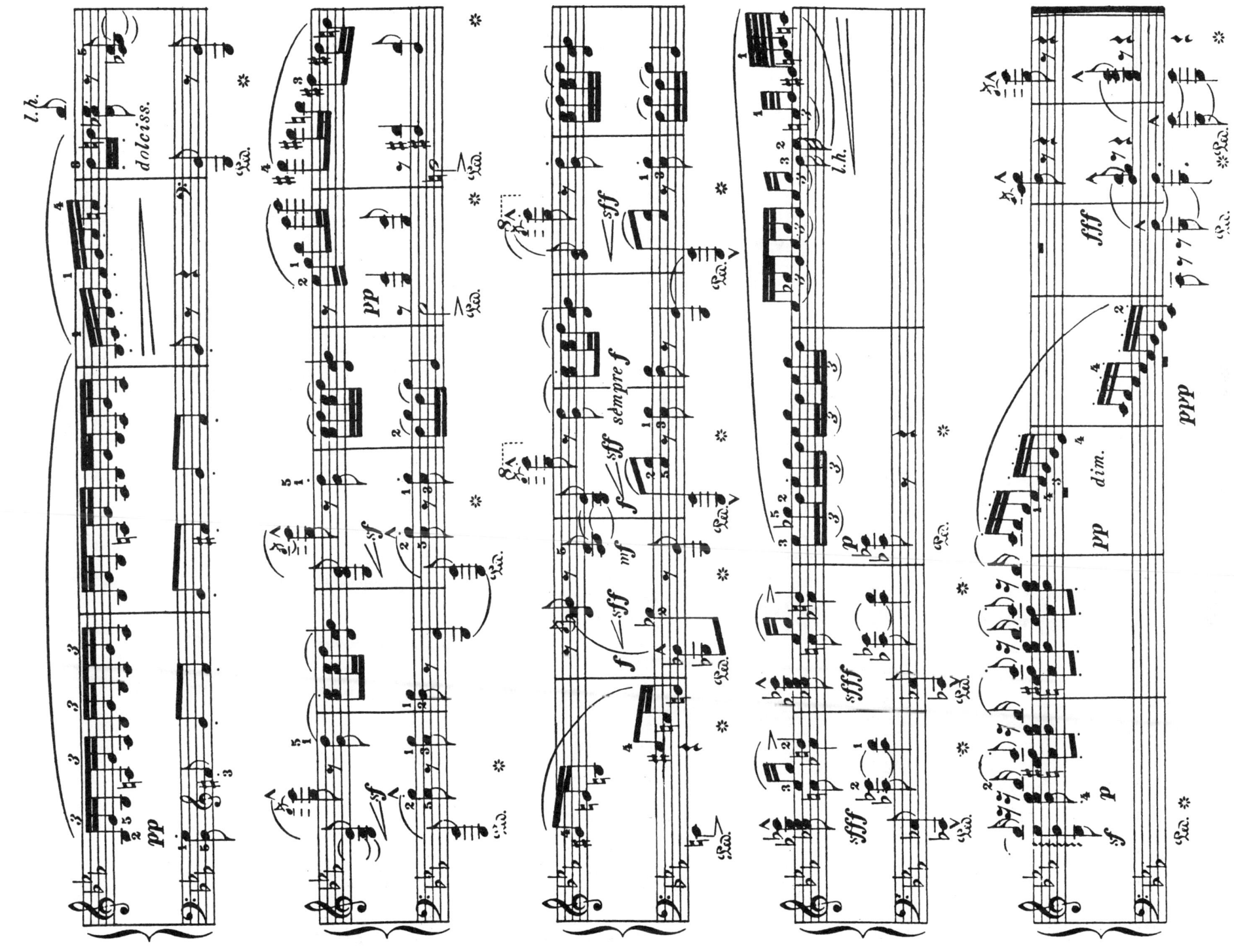

LA LISONJERA
The Flatterer
Opus 50

Moderato, molto capriccioso.

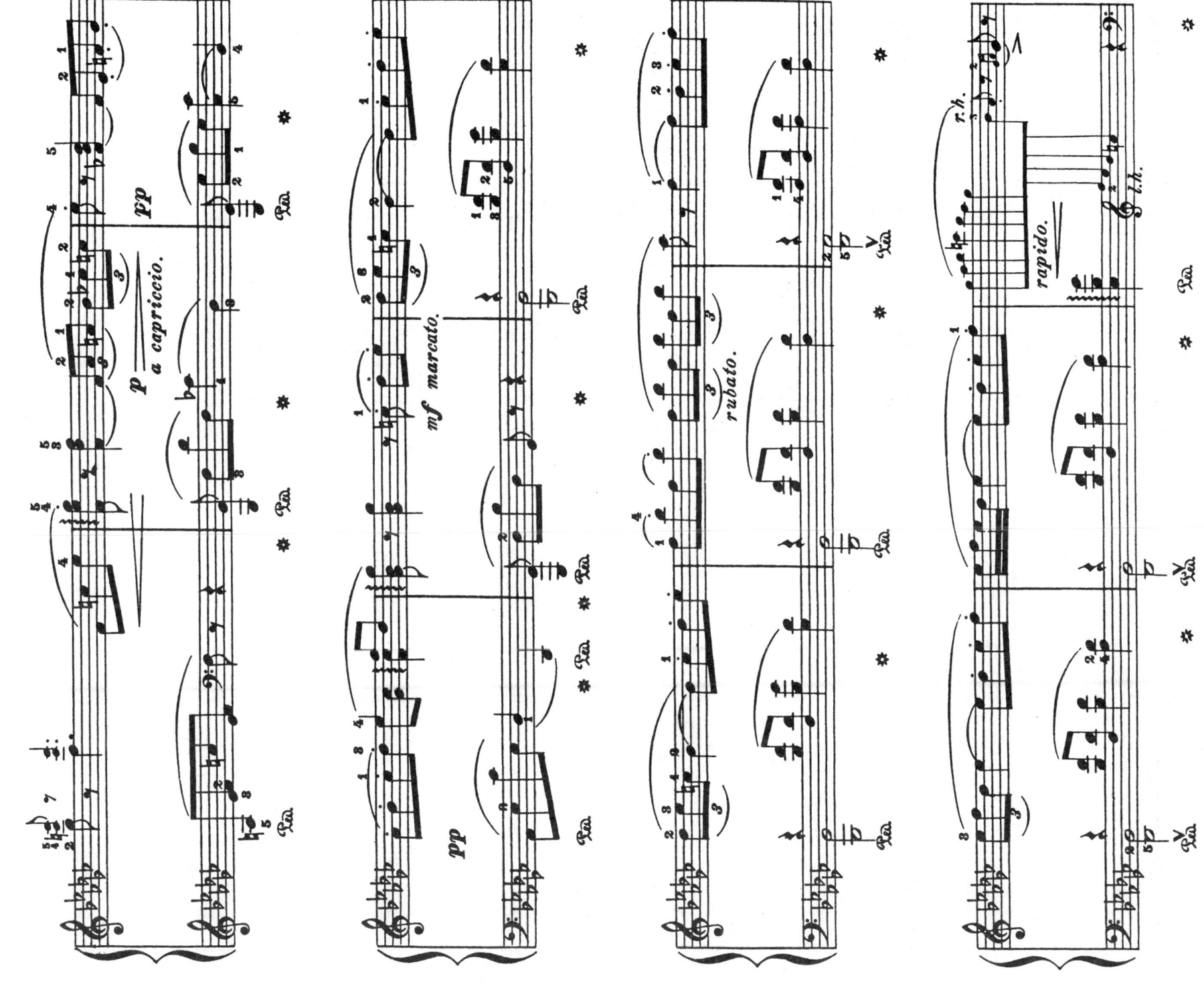

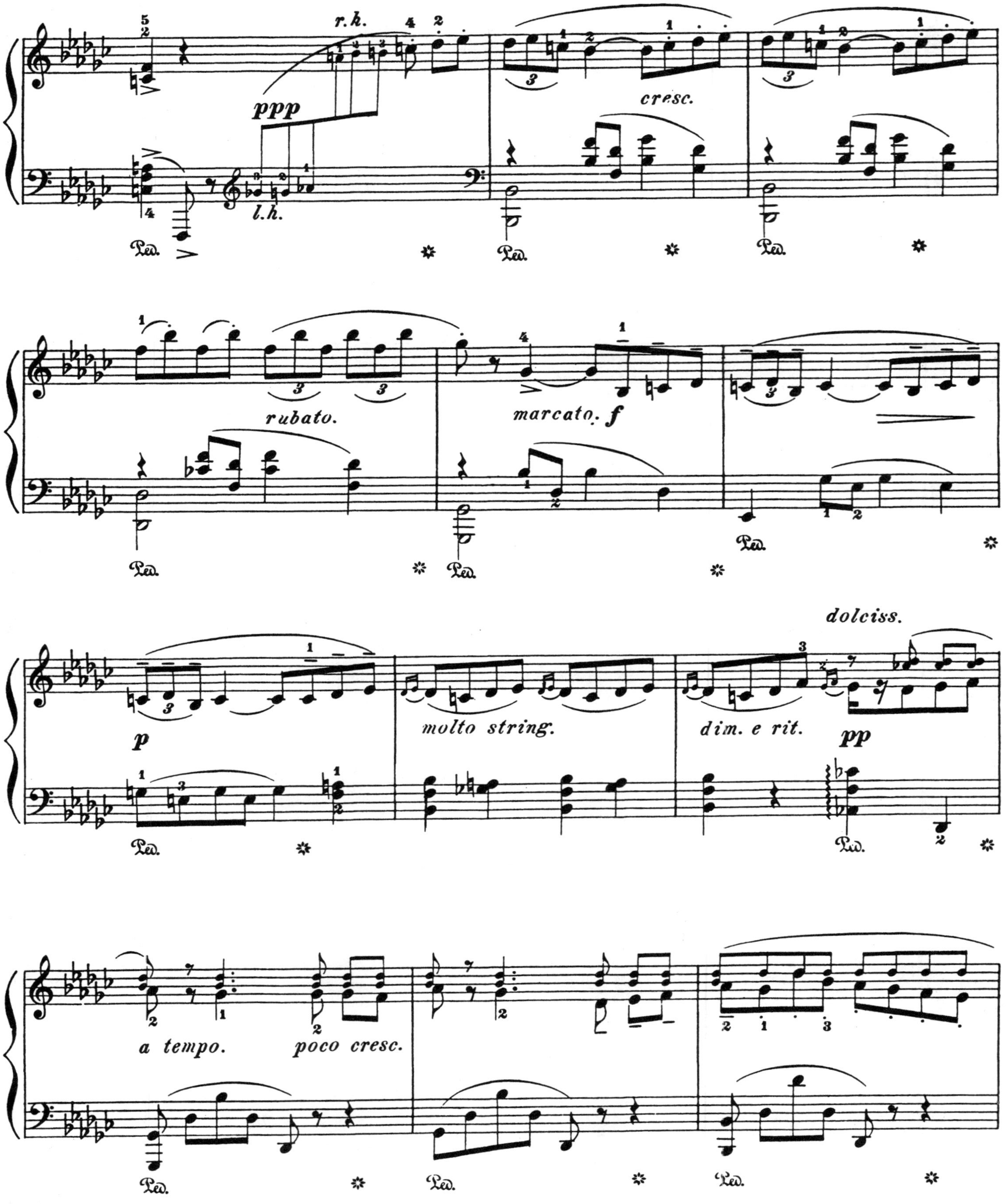
r.h.
ppp
l.h.
cresc.
rubato.
marcato. f
p
molto string.
dim. e rit.
dolciss.
pp
a tempo.
poco cresc.

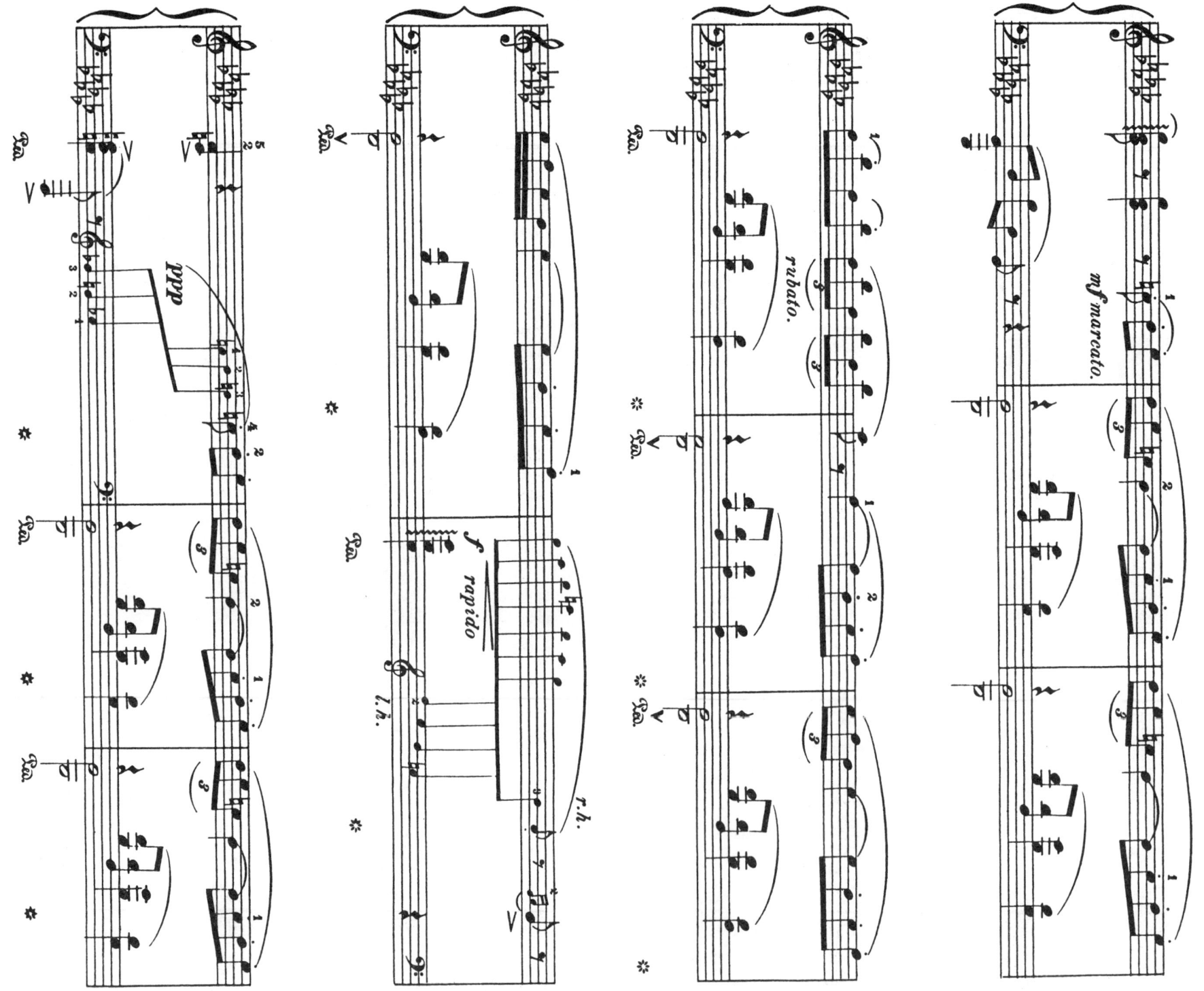

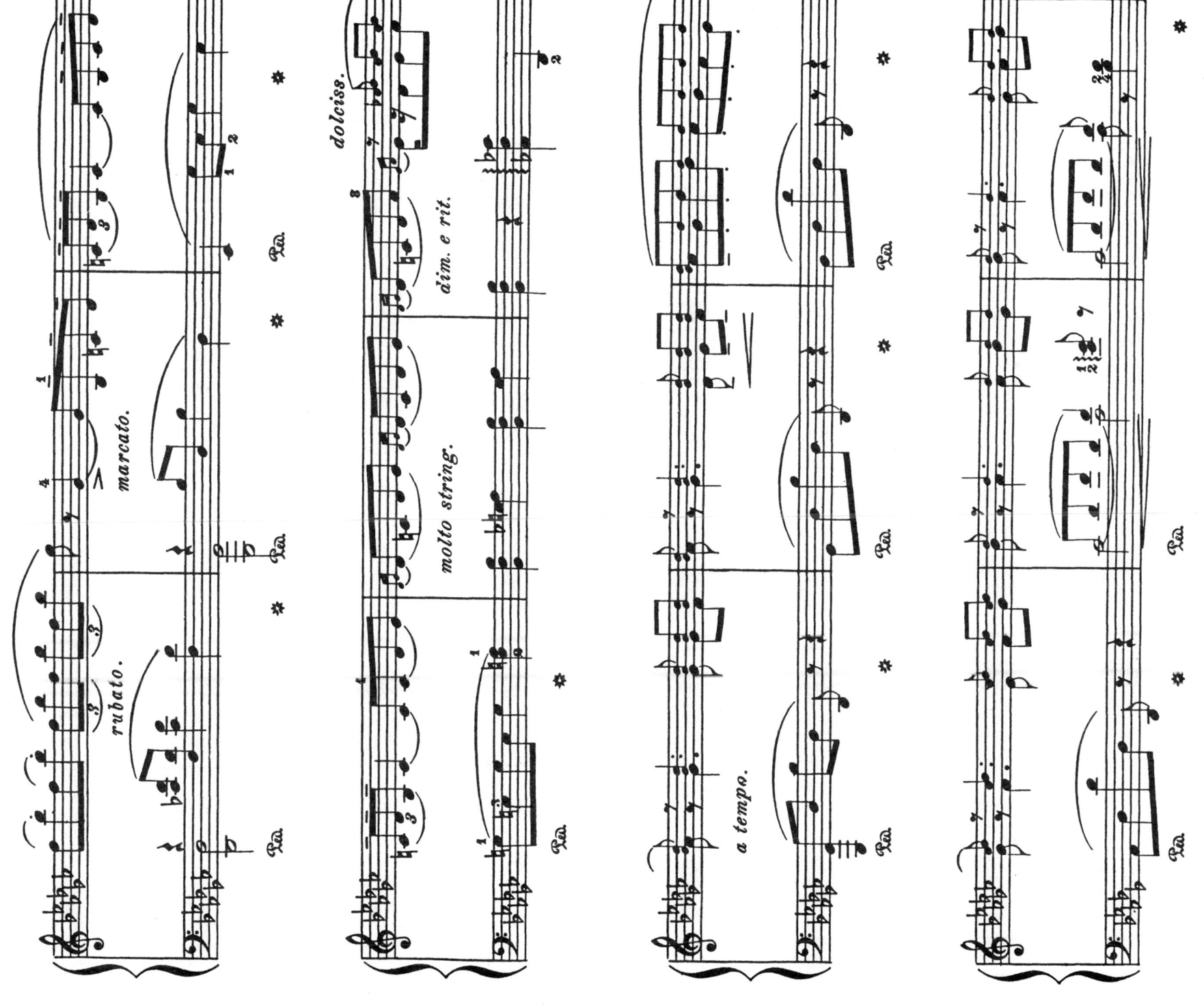

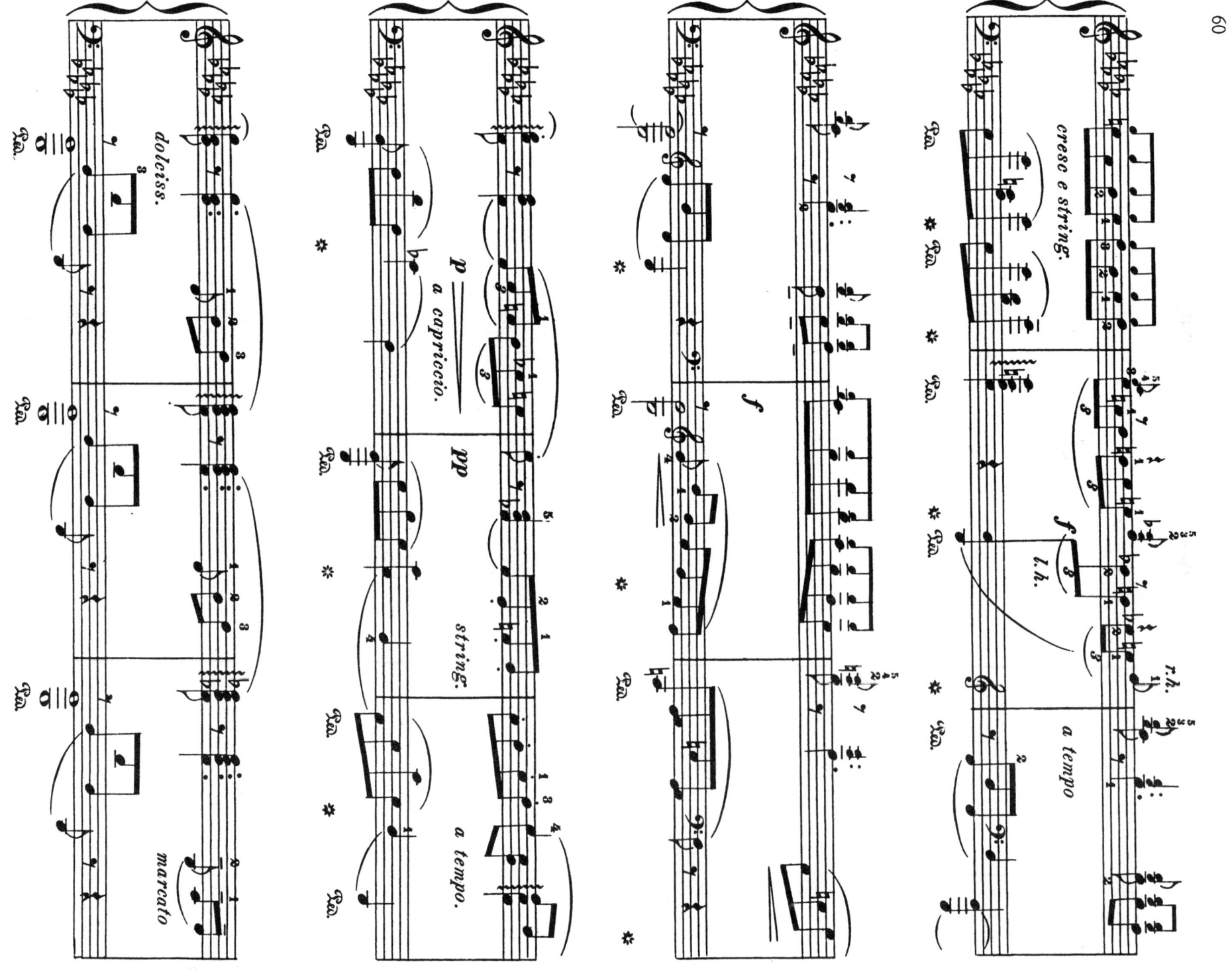

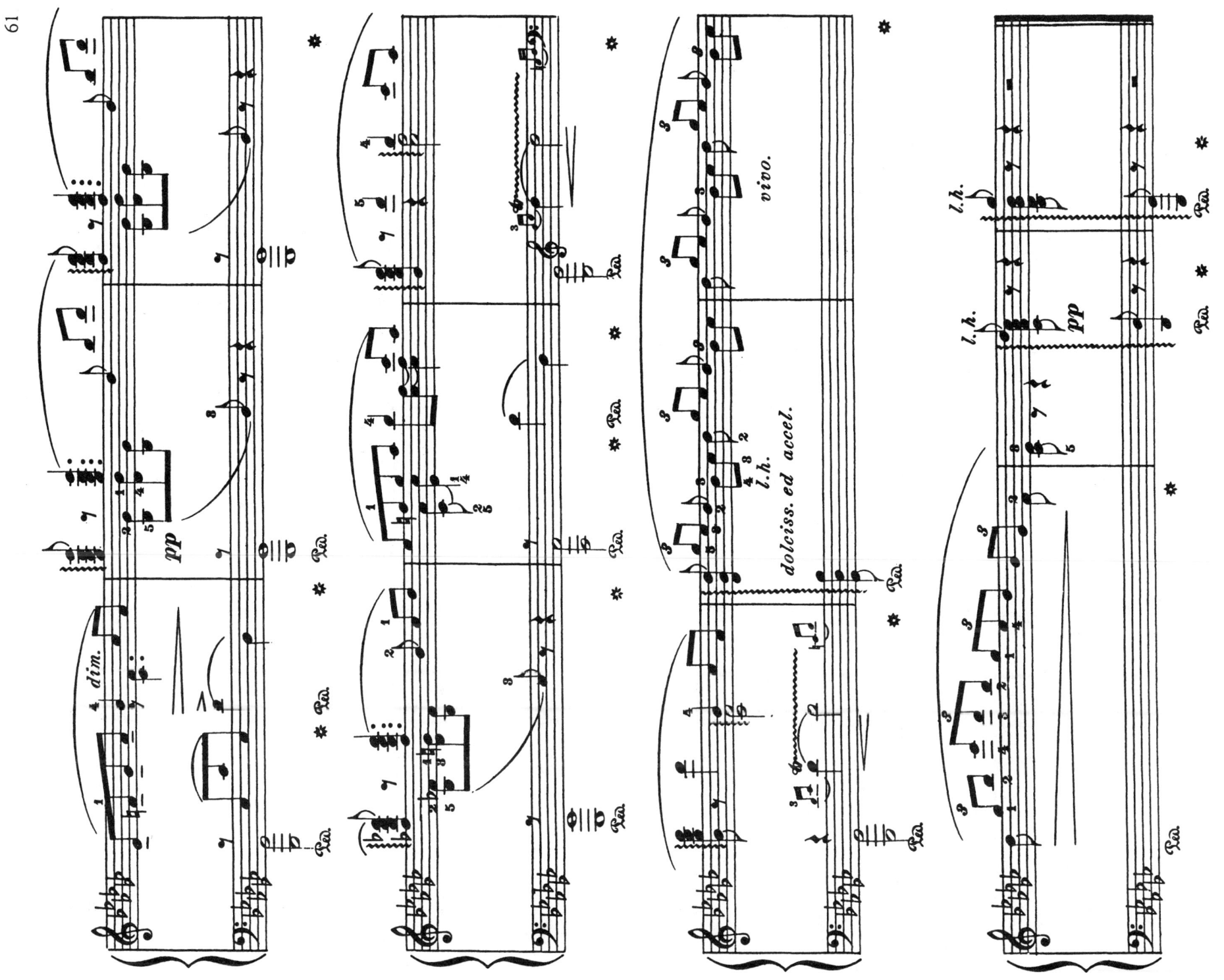

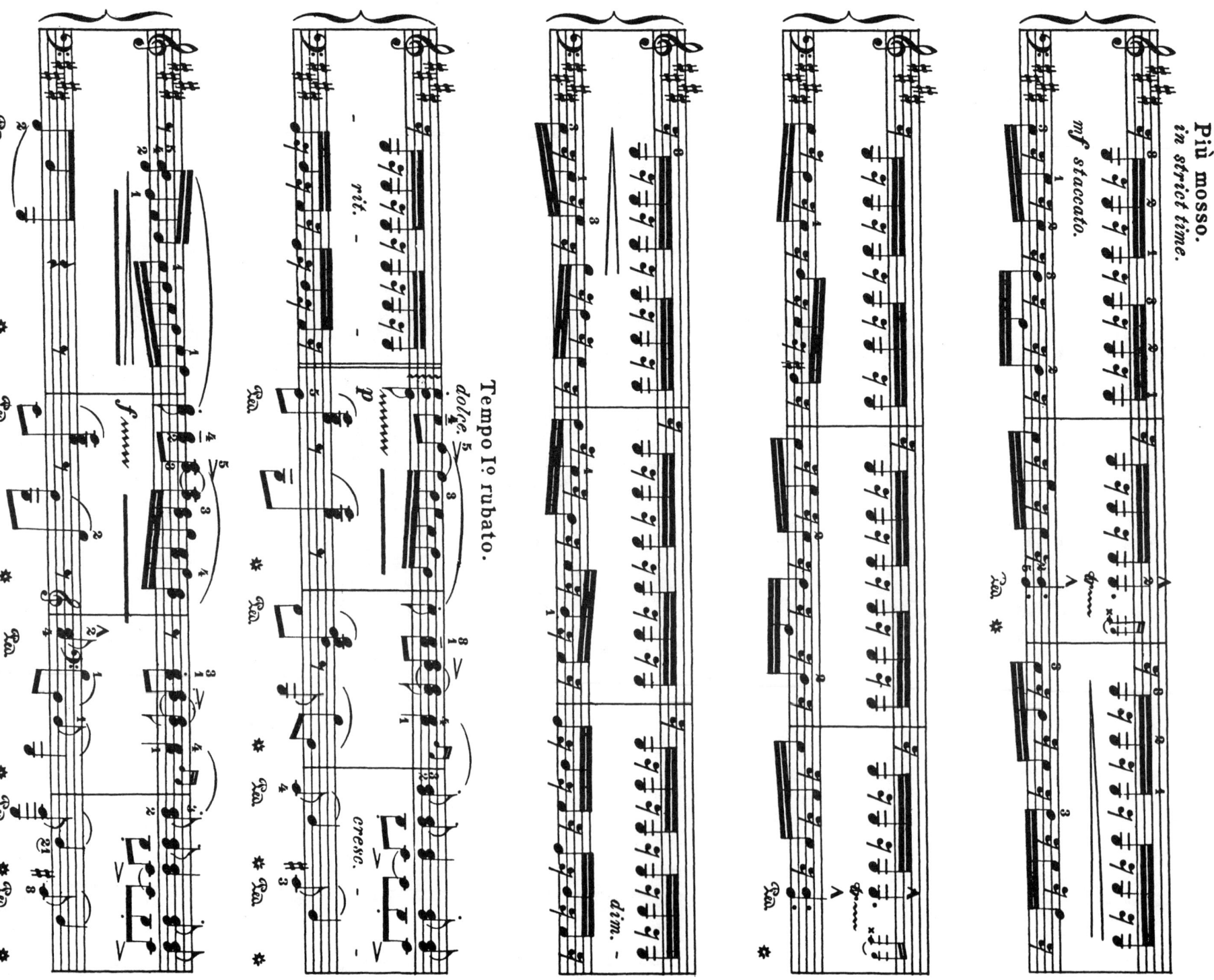

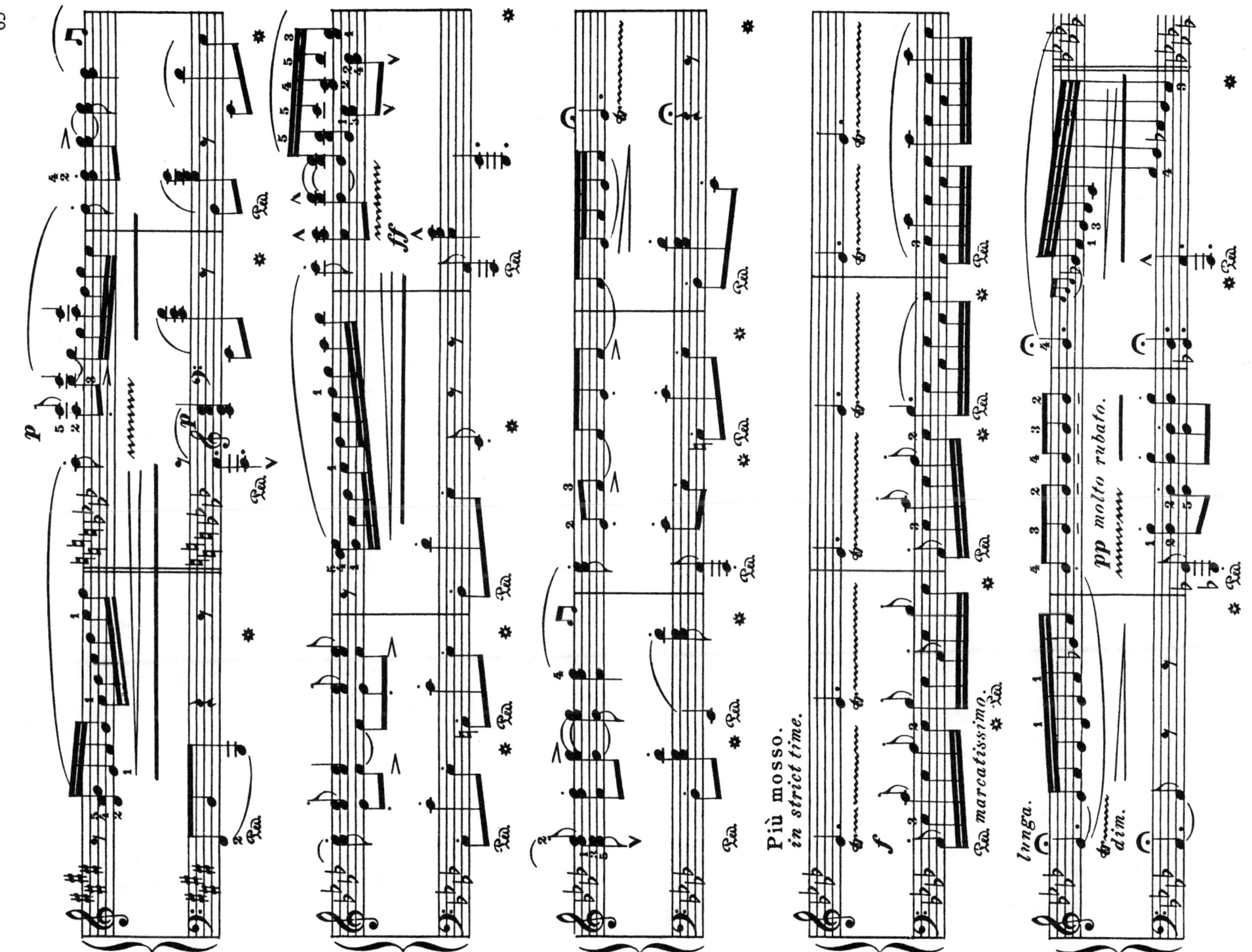

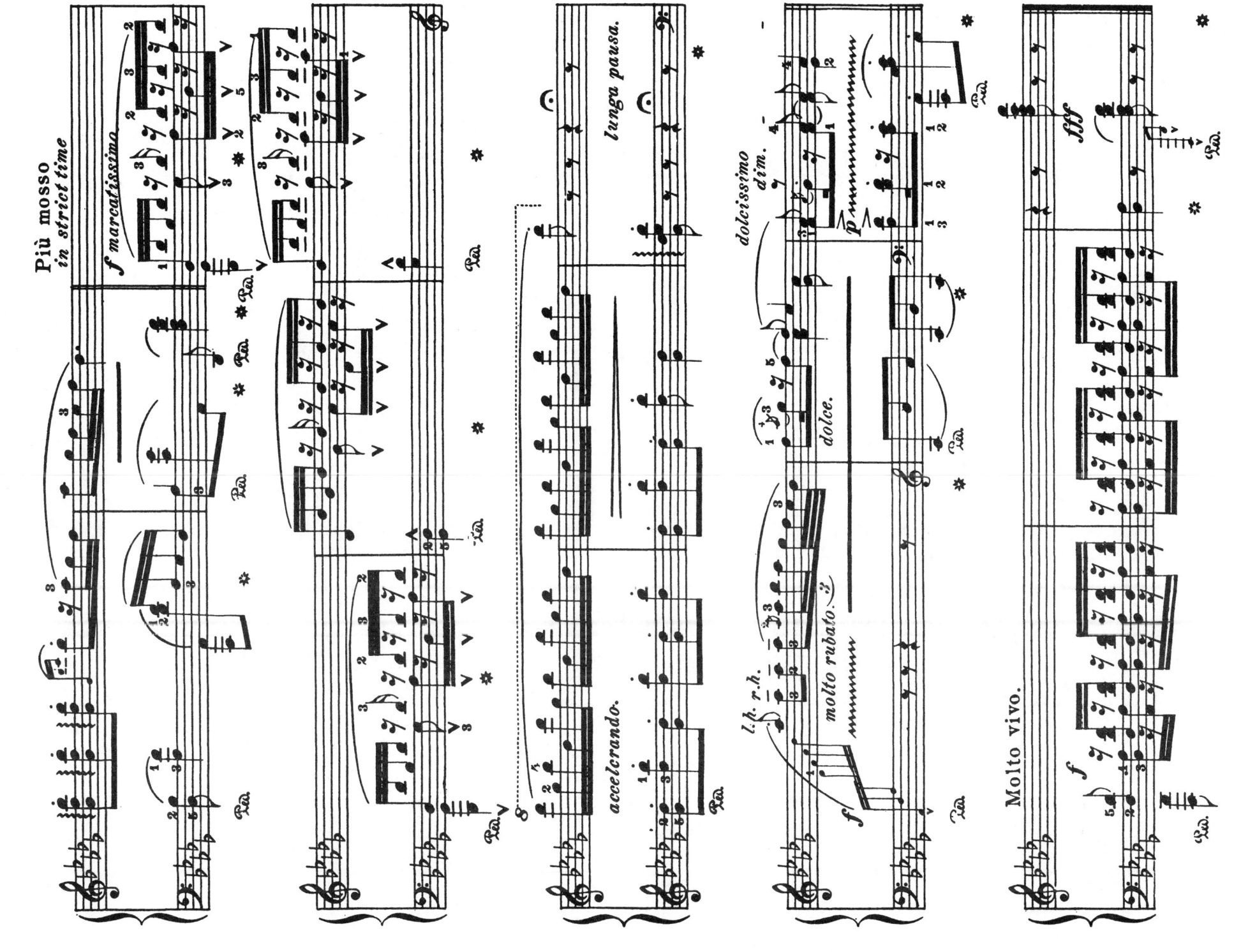

LES SYLVAINS
The Fauns
Opus 60

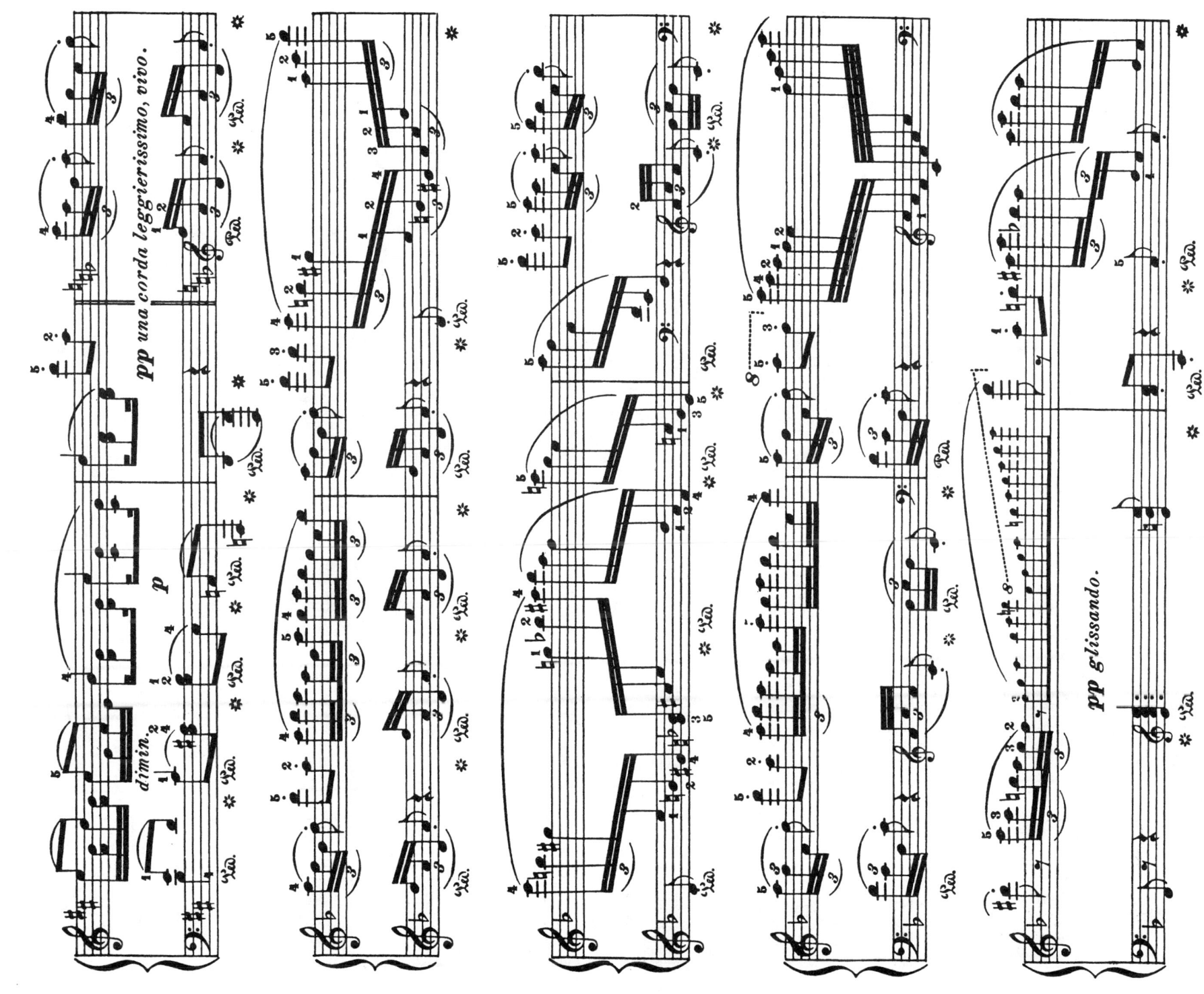

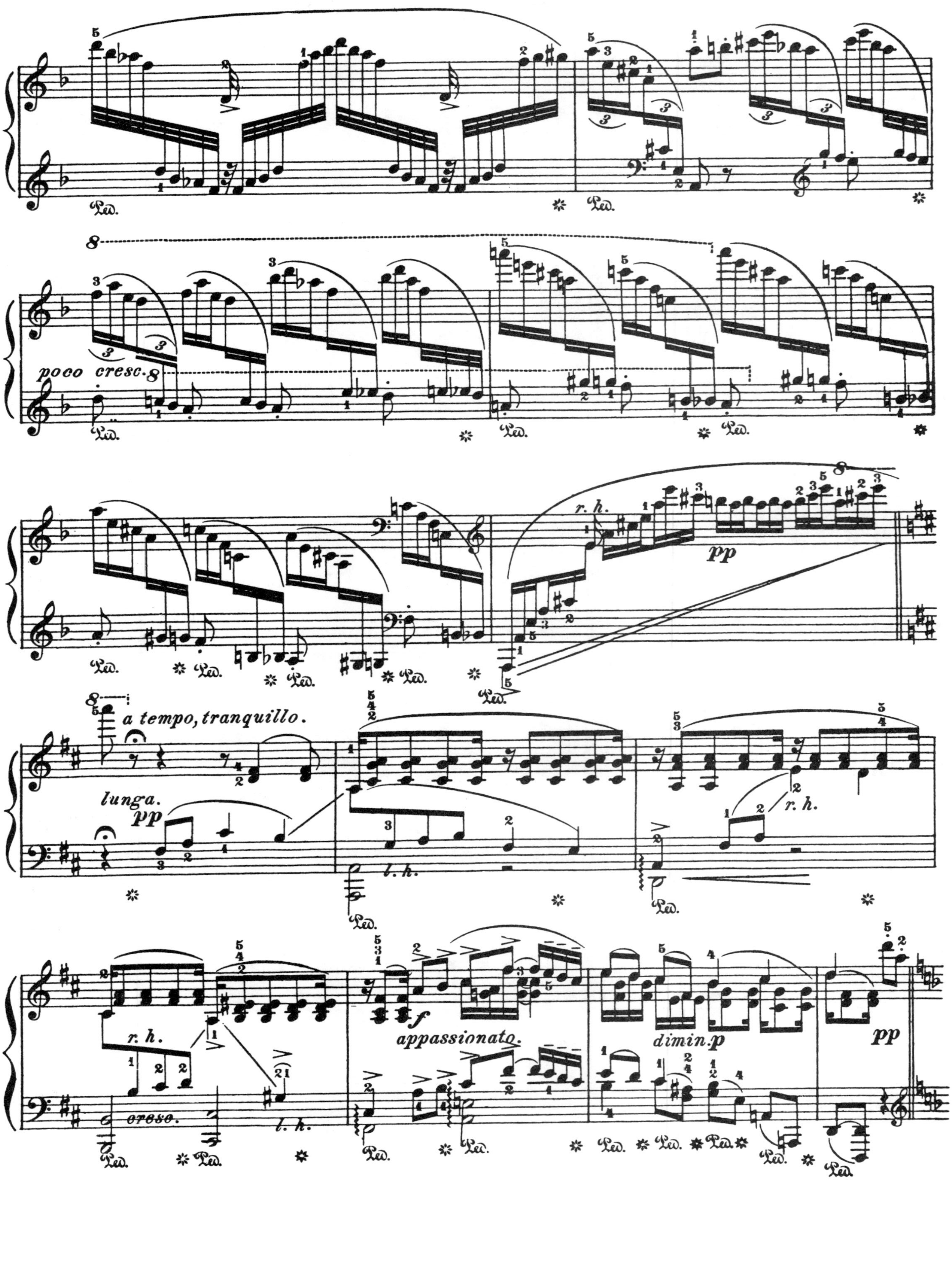
poco cresc.
r. h.
pp
a tempo, tranquillo.
lunga.
pp
l. h.
r. h.
r. h.
cresc.
l. h.
f
appassionato.
dimin. p
pp

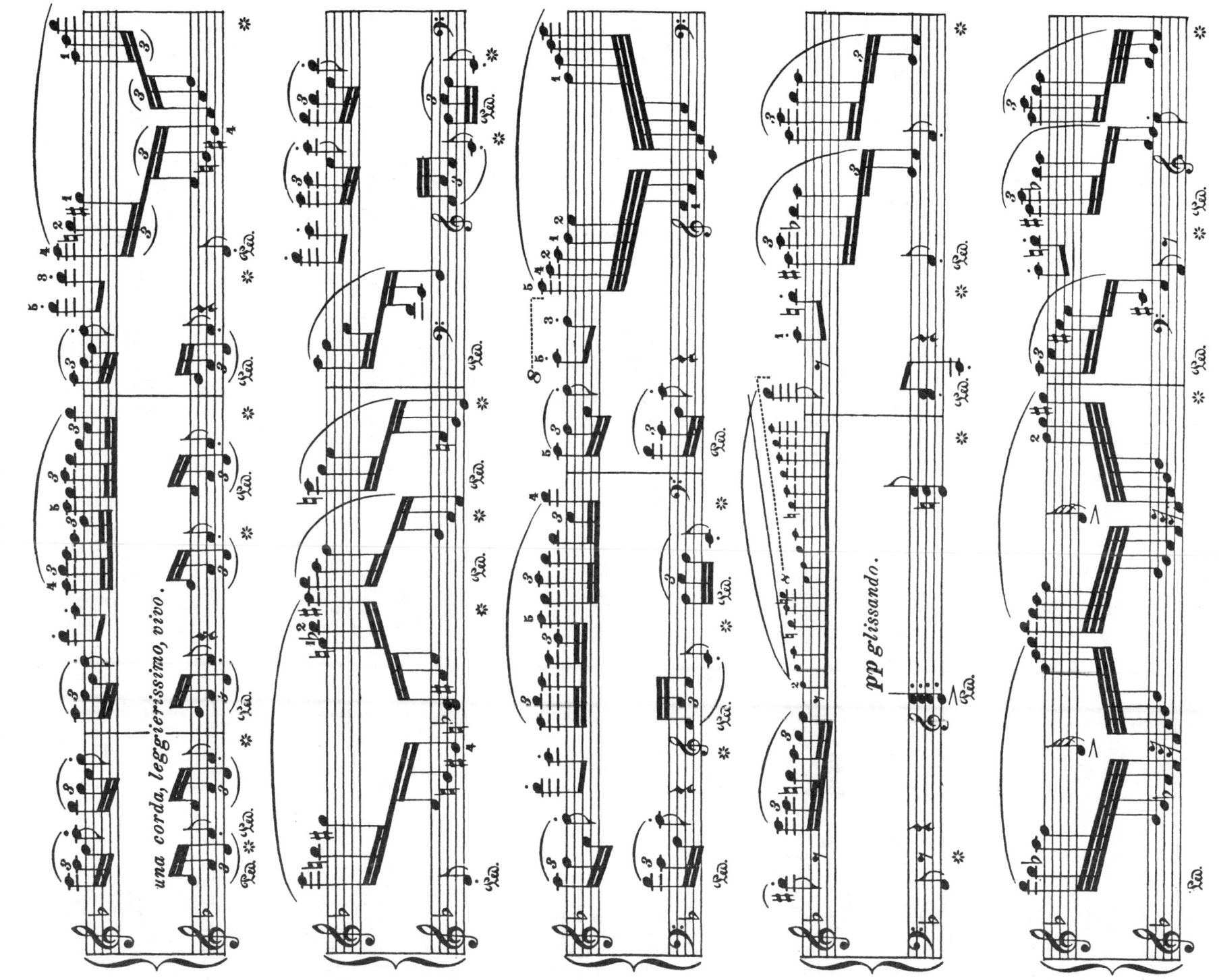

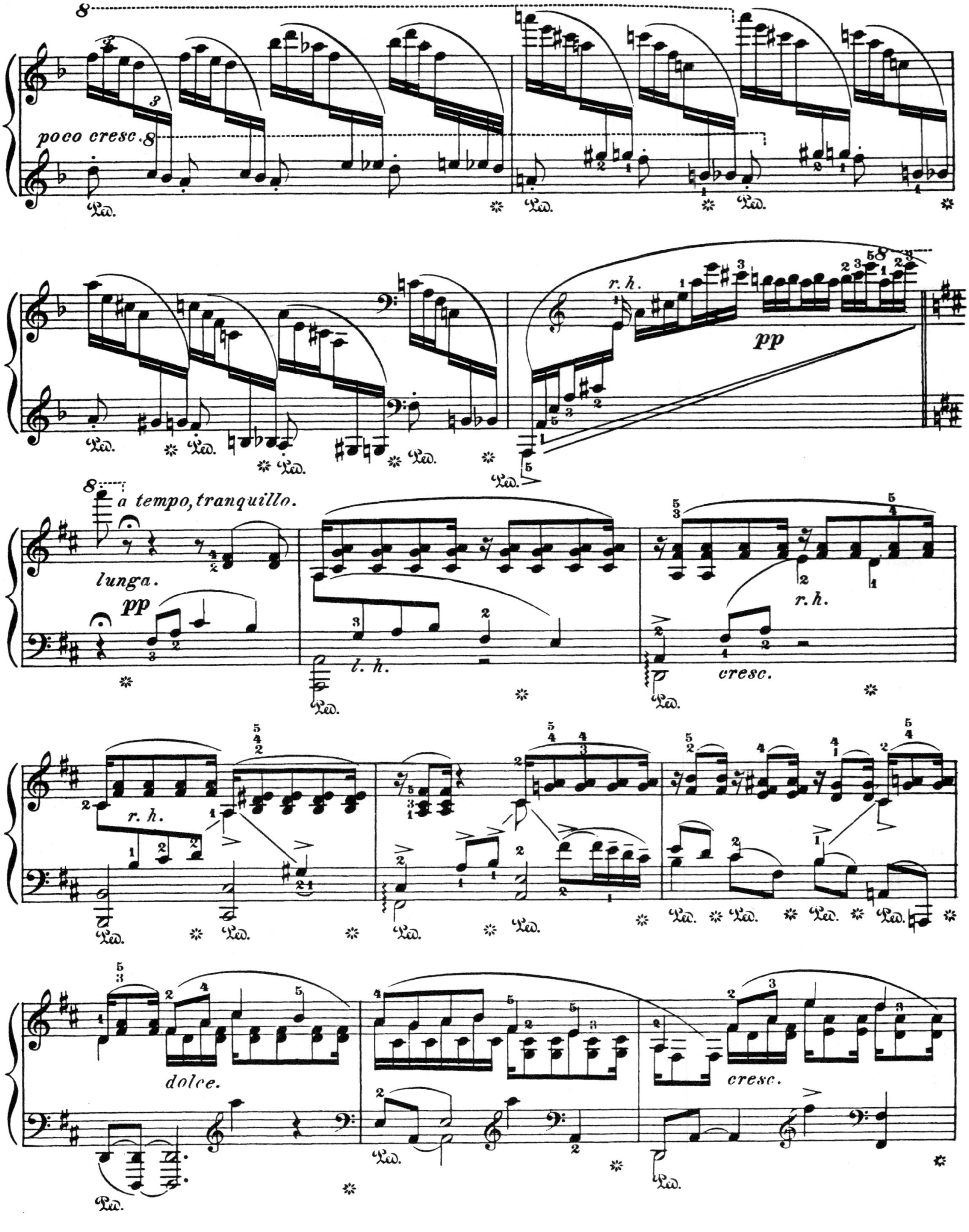
poco cresc.
r. h.
pp
a tempo, tranquillo.
lunga.
pp
l. h.
r. h.
cresc.
r. h.
dolce.
cresc.

ARABESQUE
Opus 61

Allegro risoluto. ($\quarternote$ = 152.)

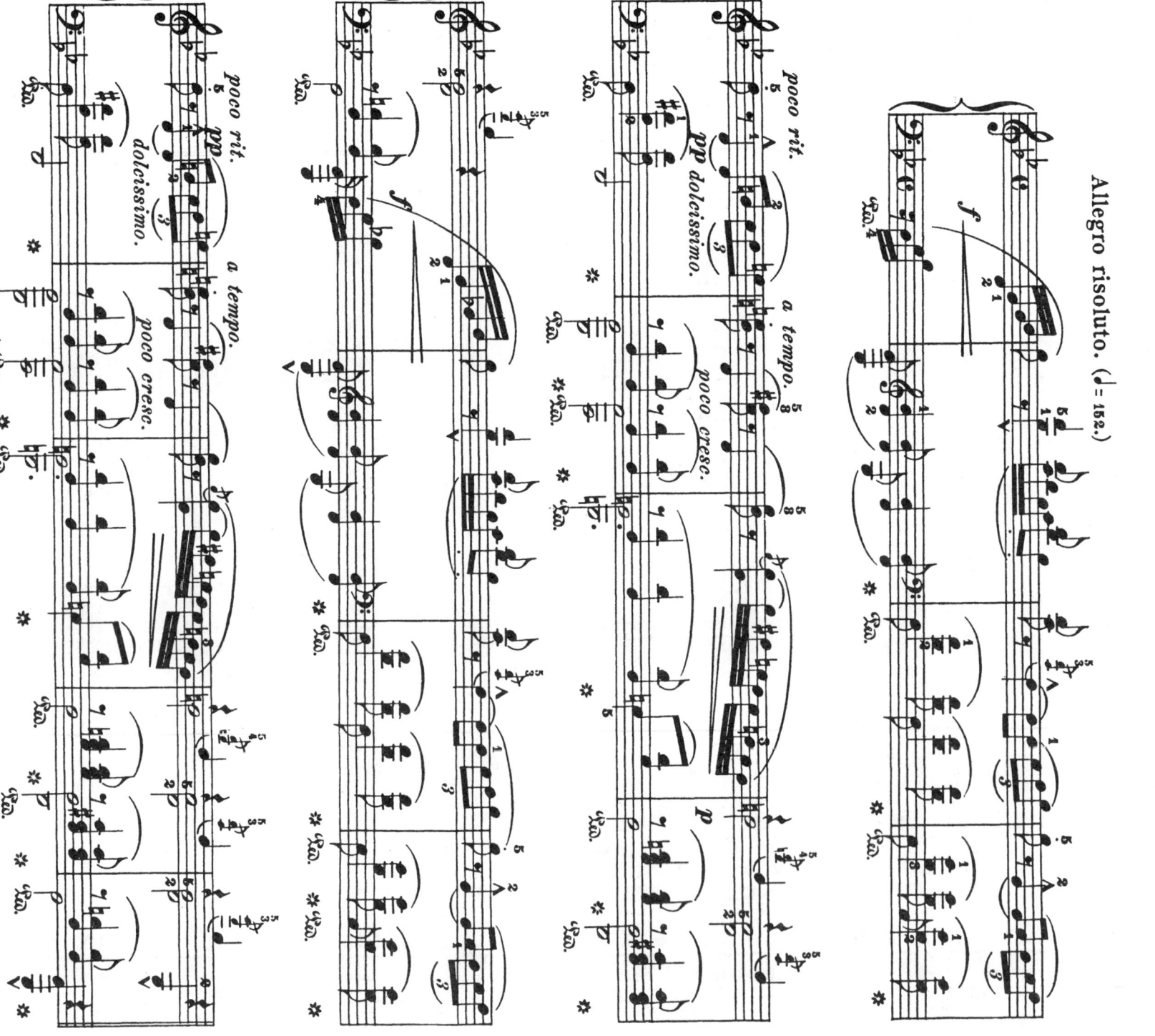

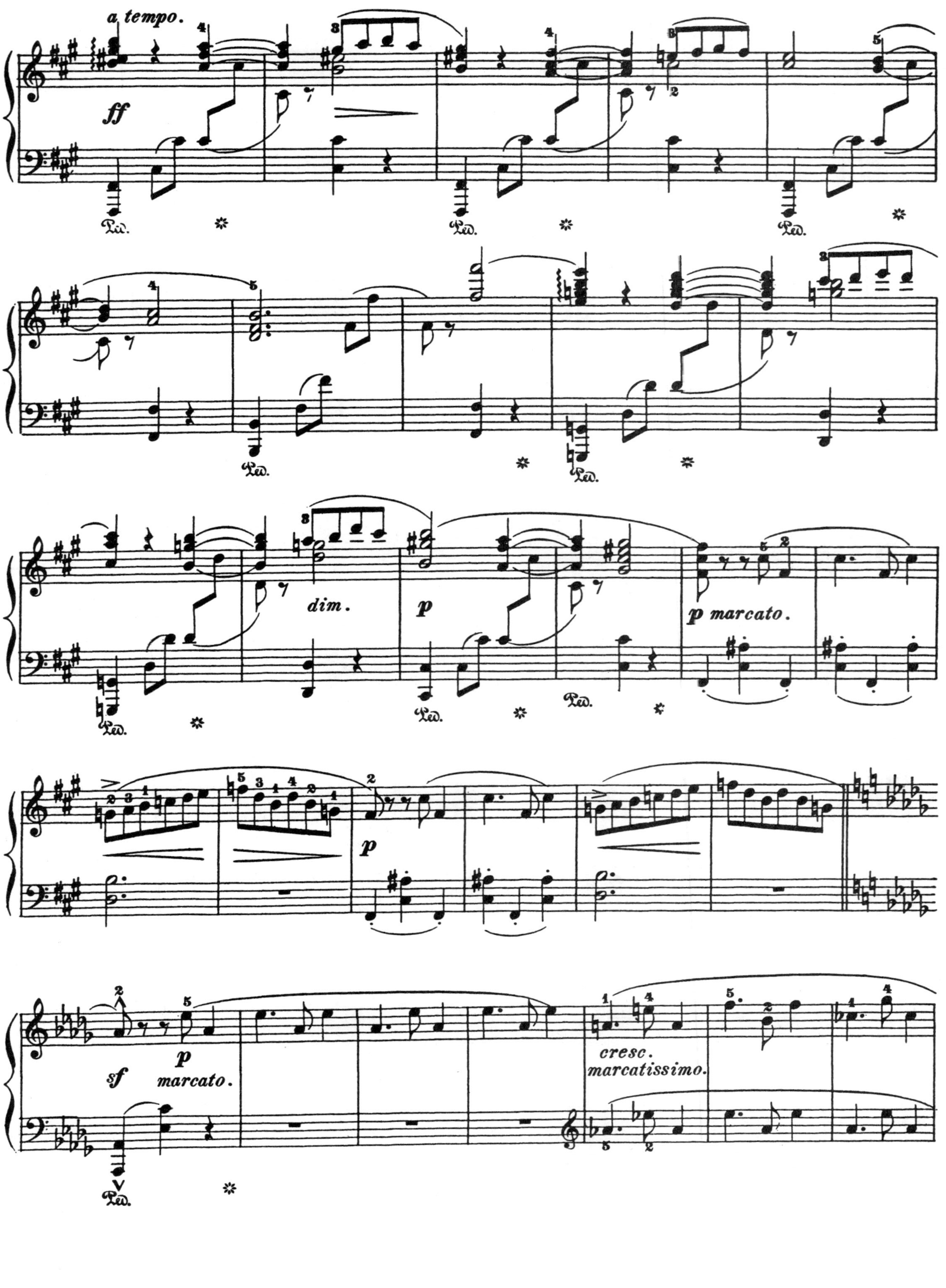
a tempo.
ff
dim.
p
p marcato.
p
sf
p
marcato.
cresc.
marcatissimo.

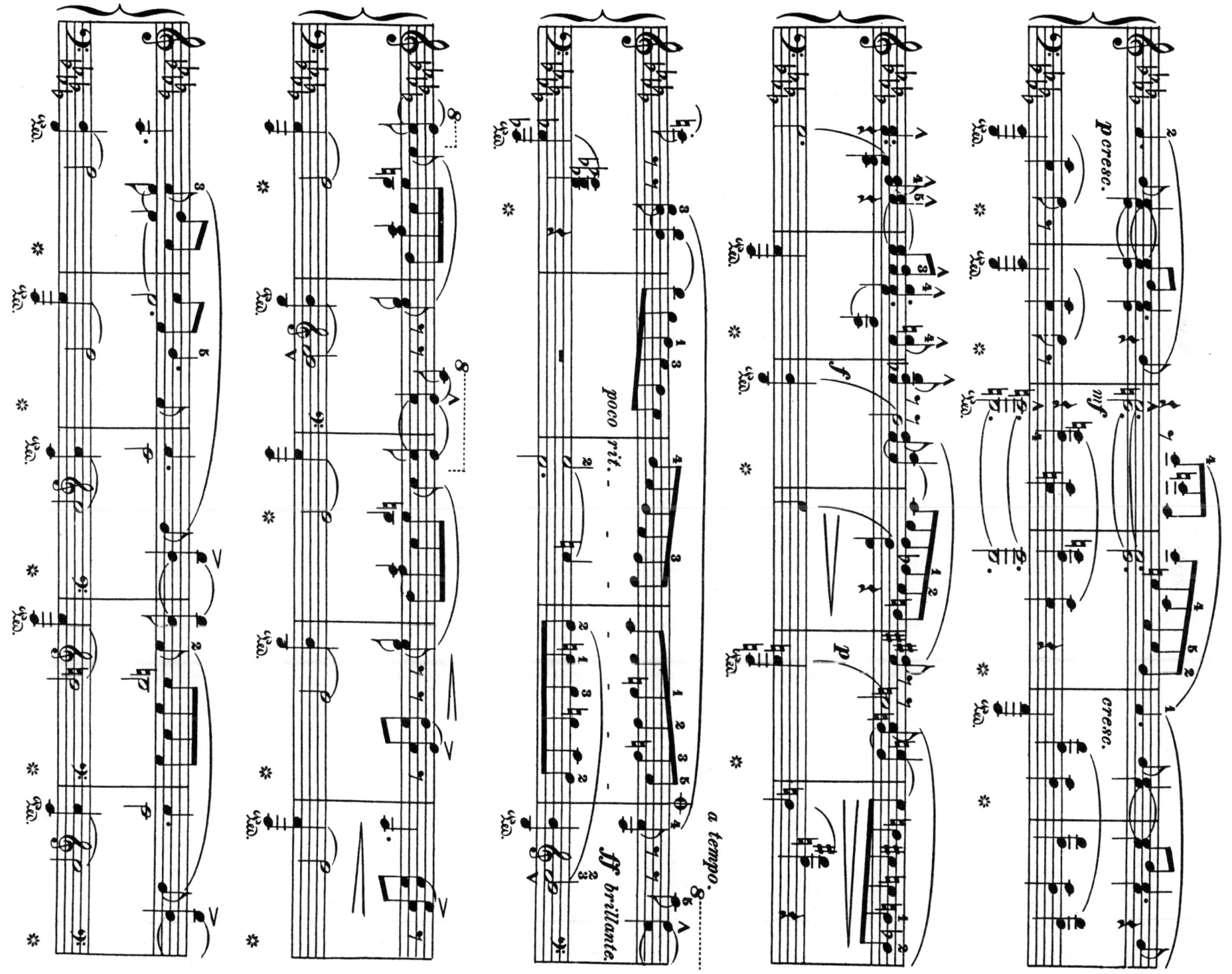

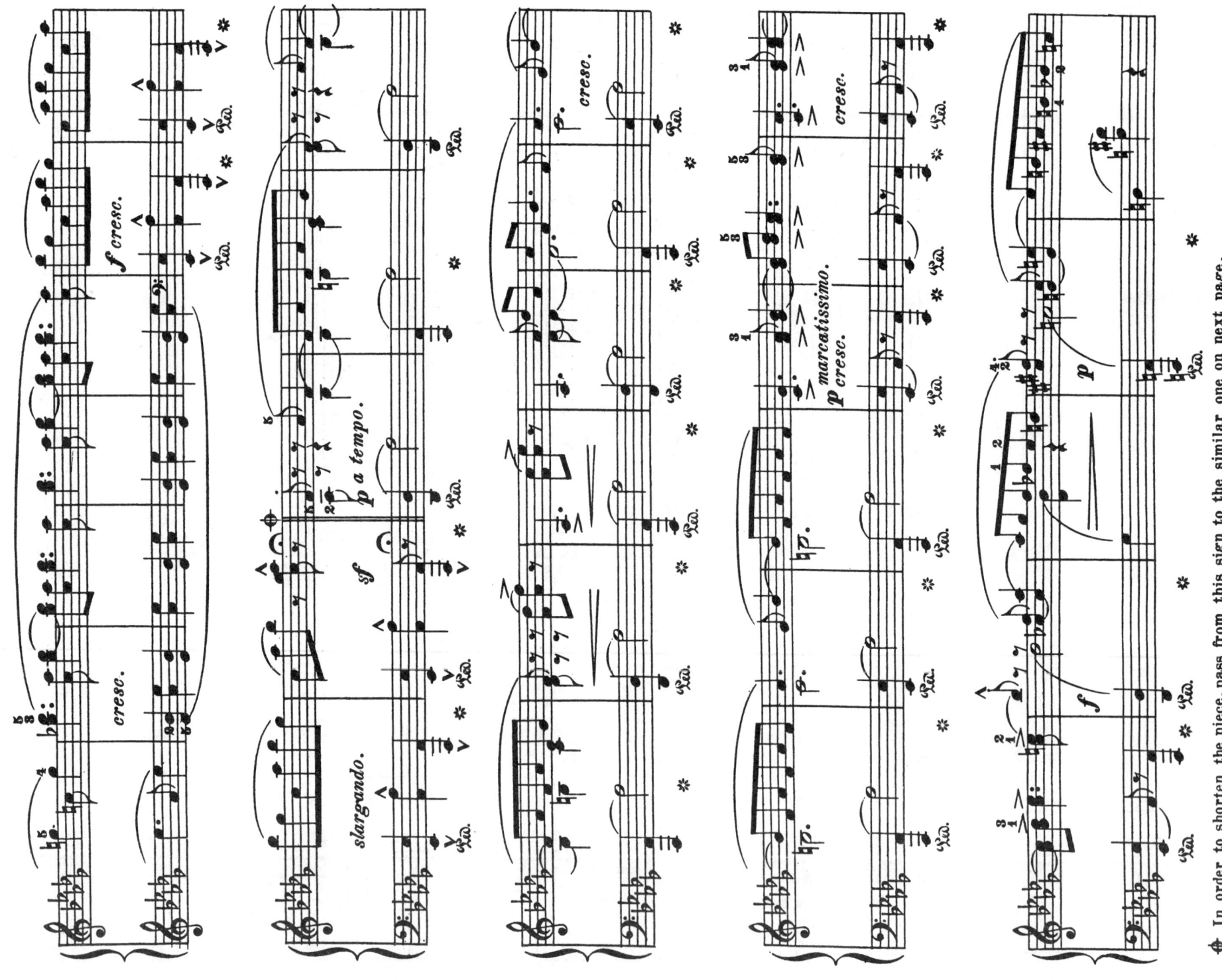

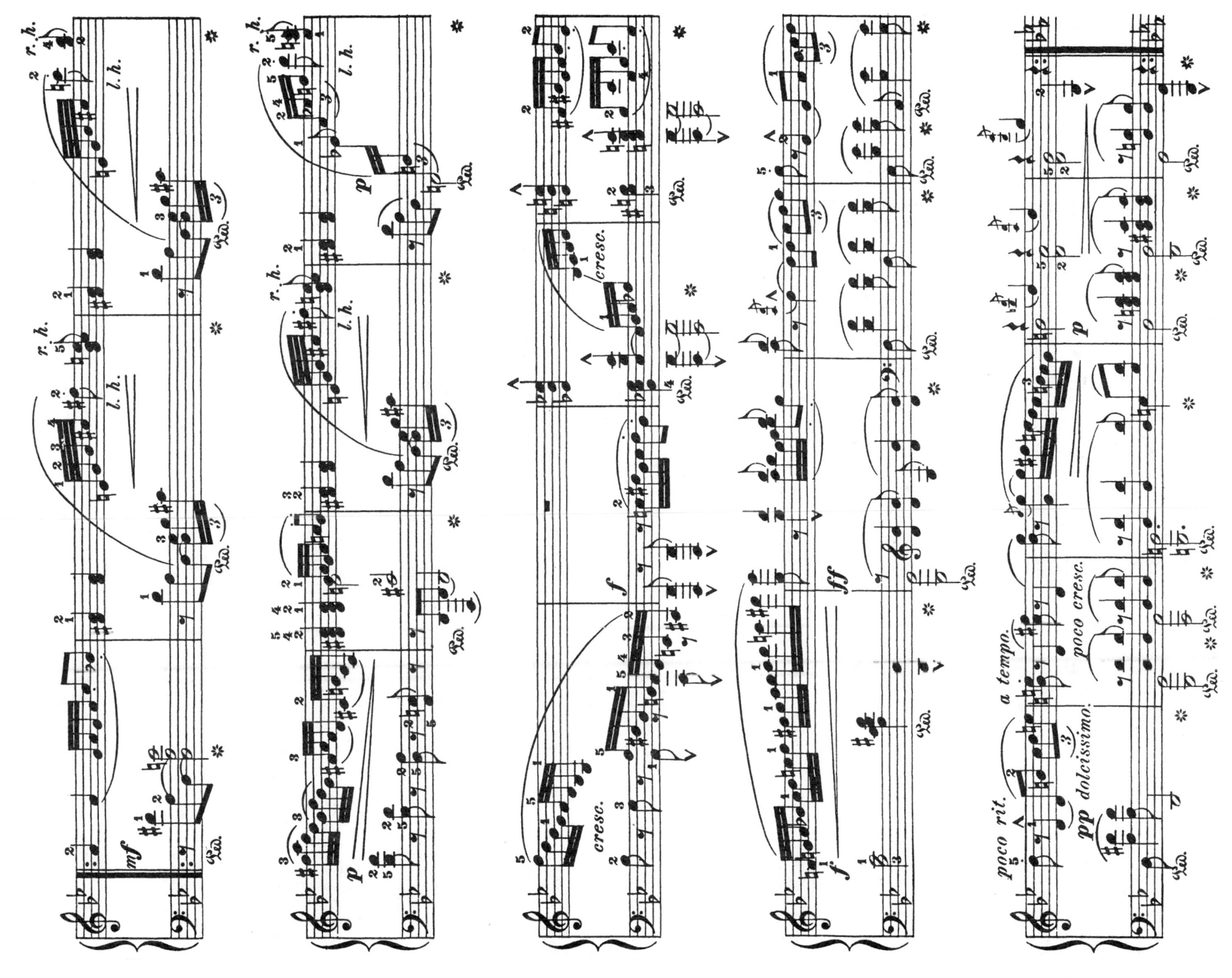

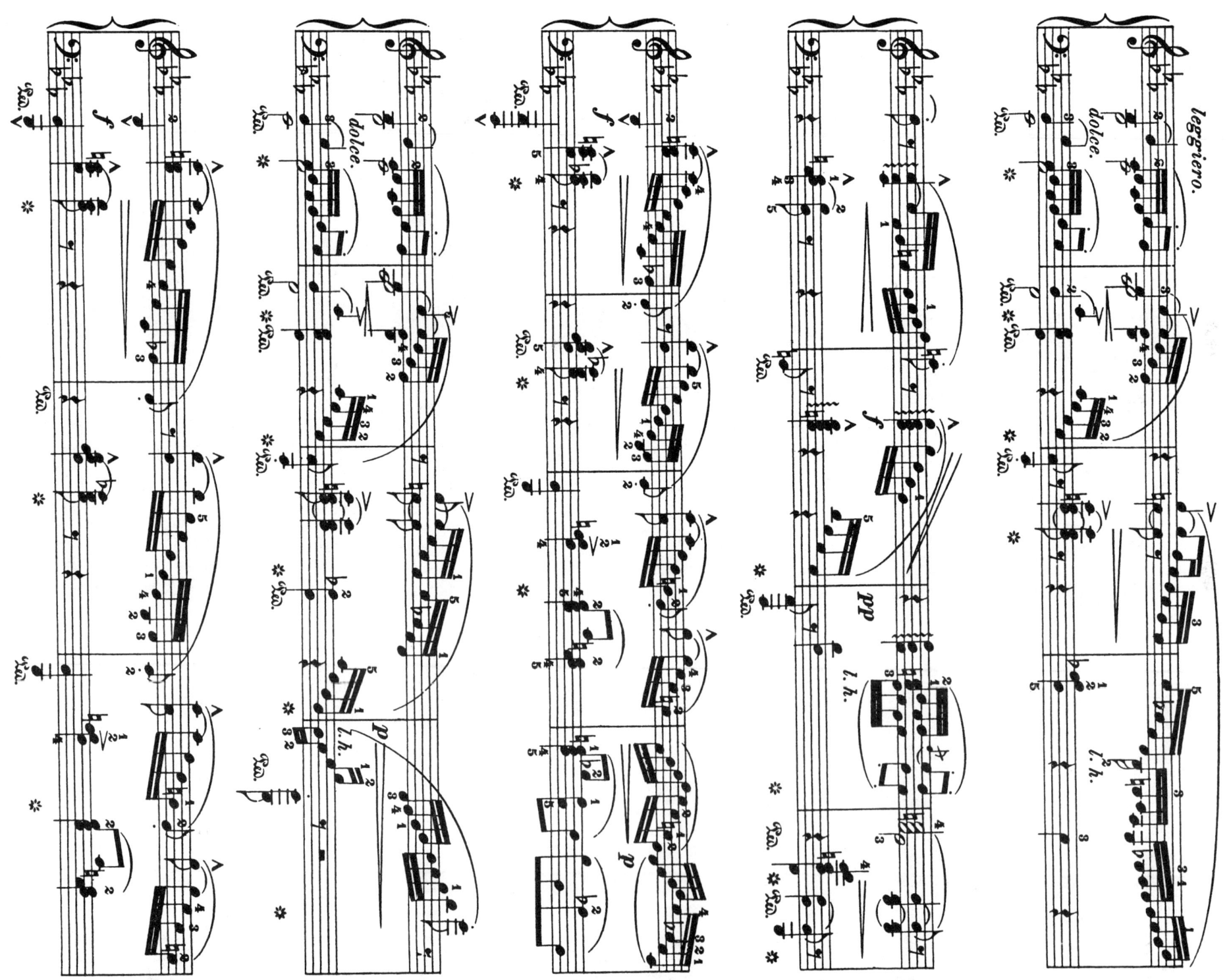

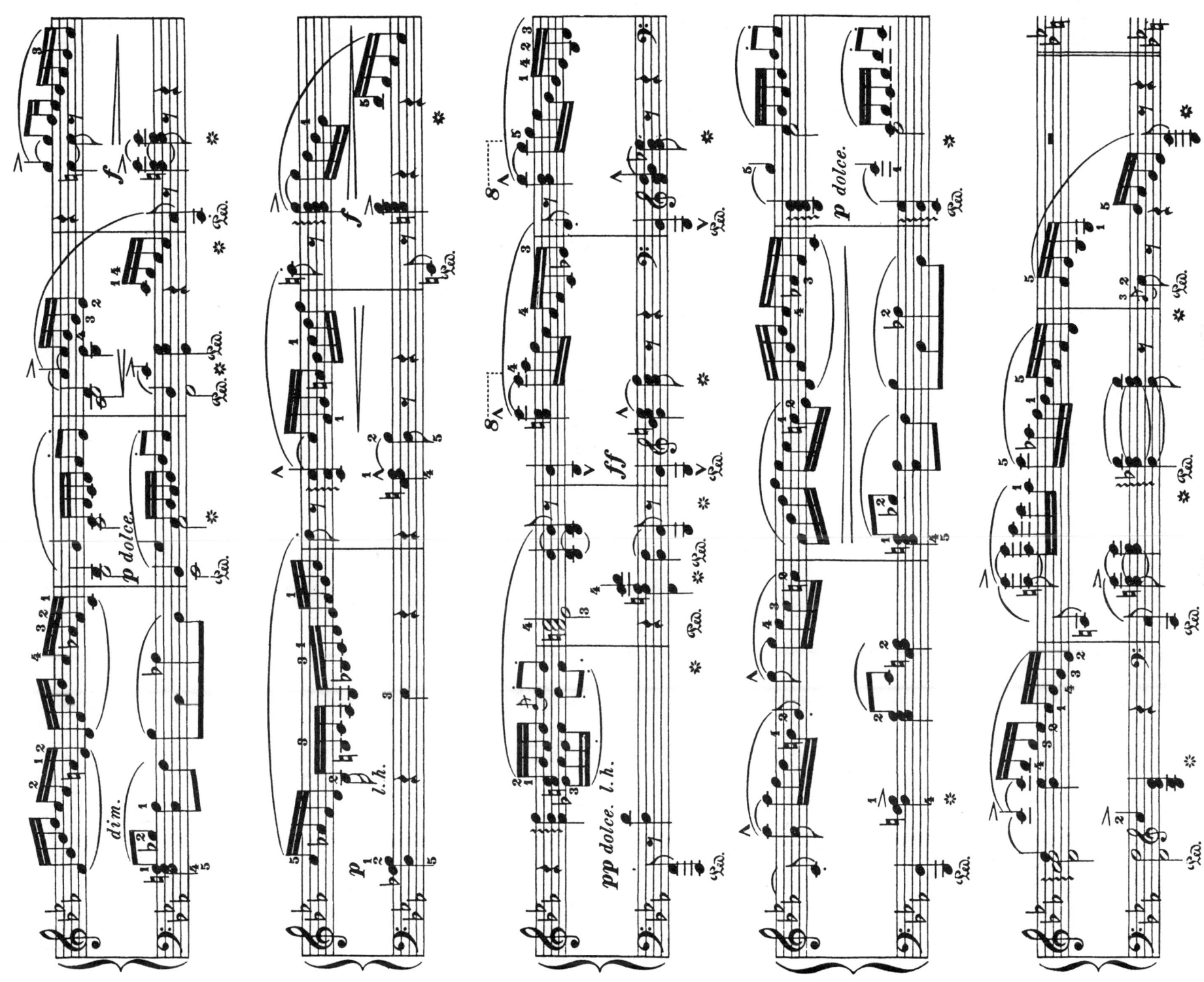

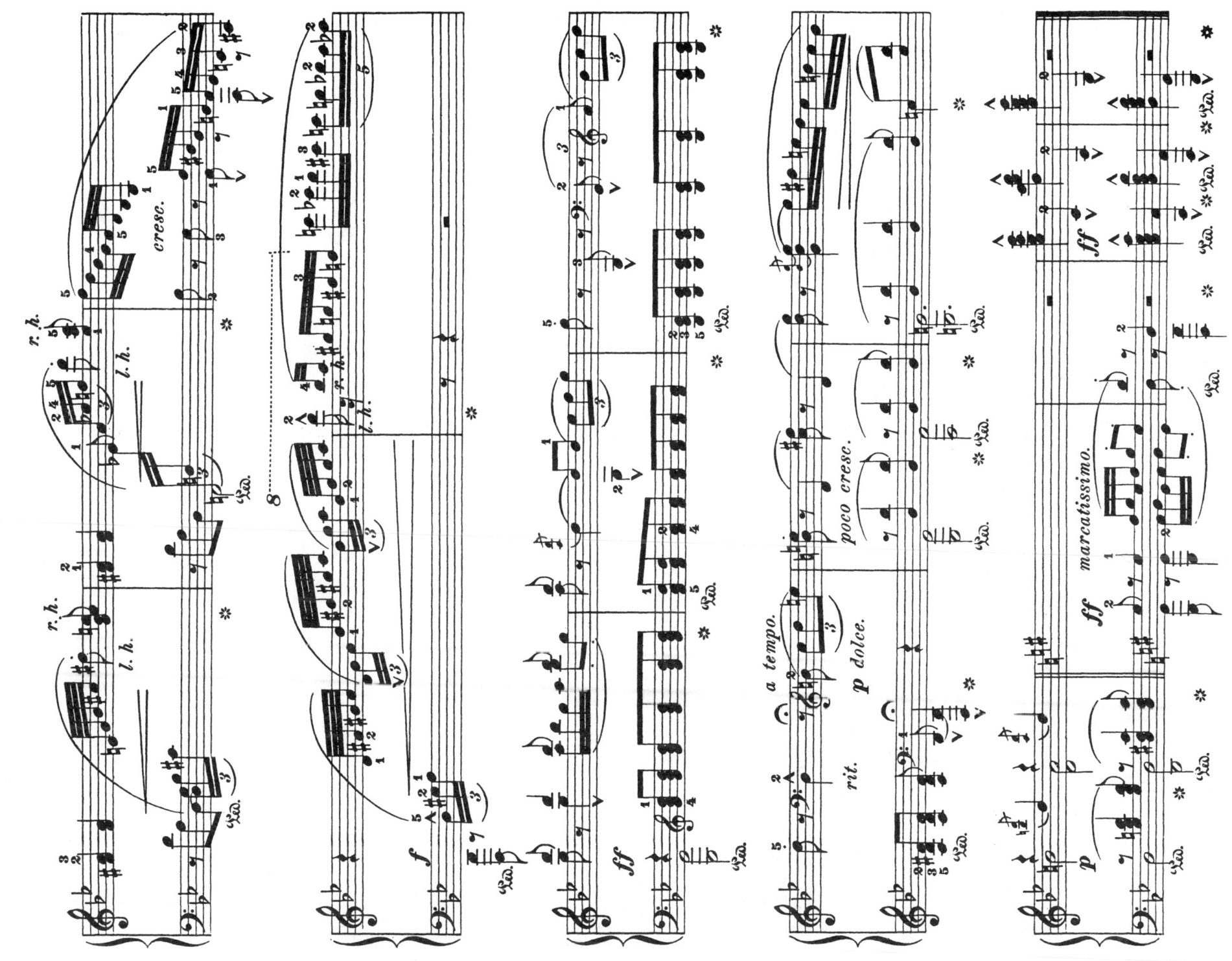

VALSE-CAPRICE
Opus 33

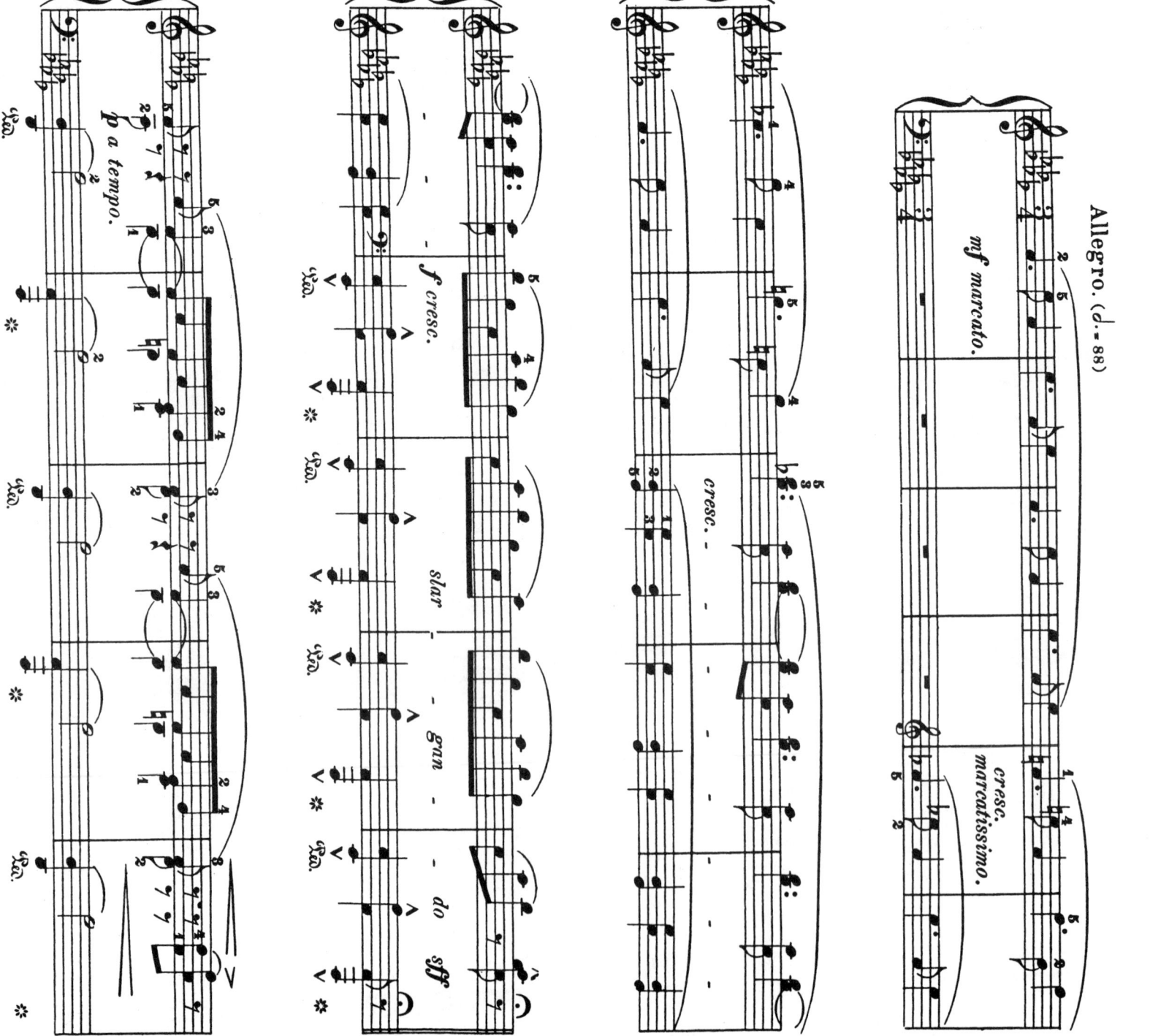

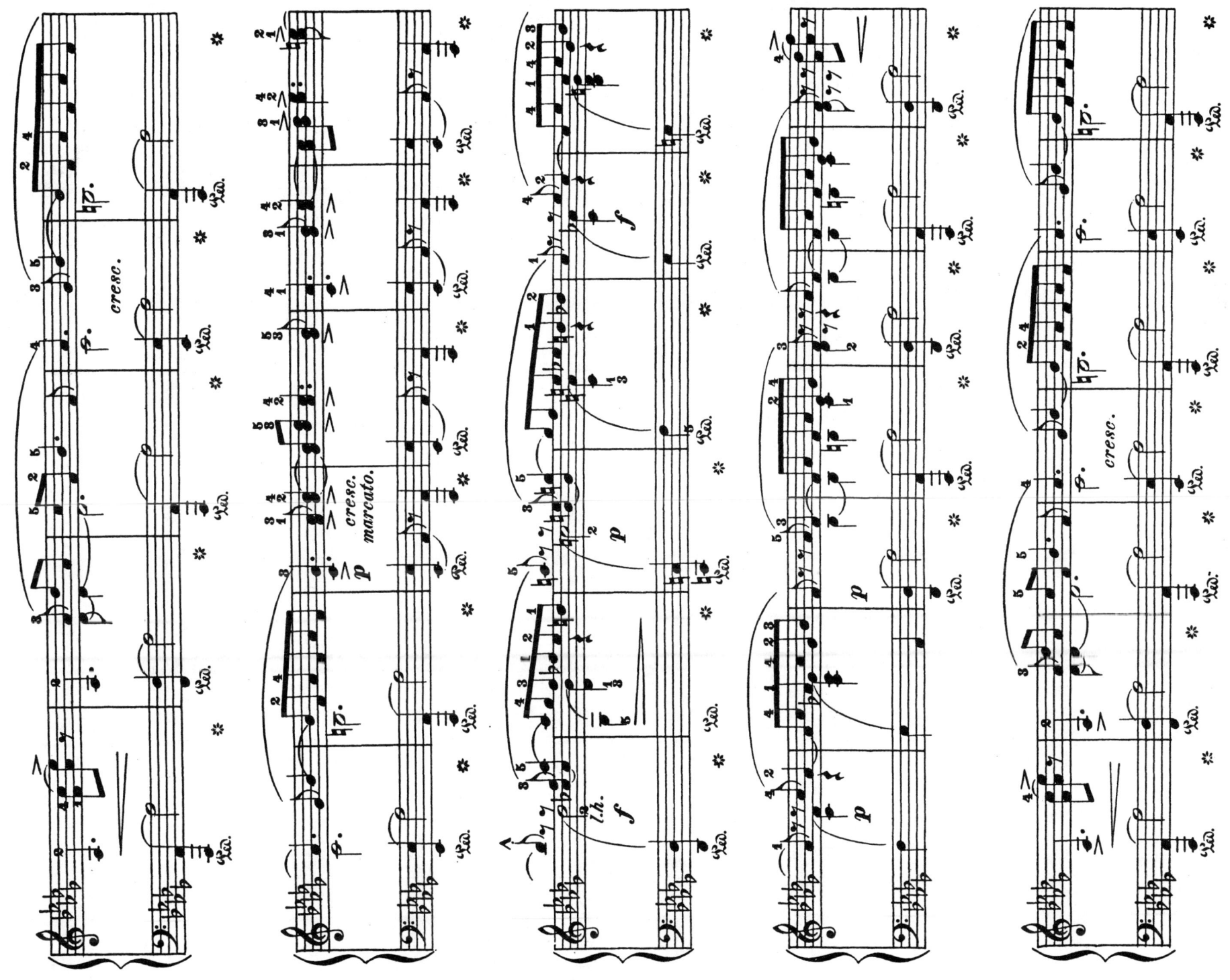

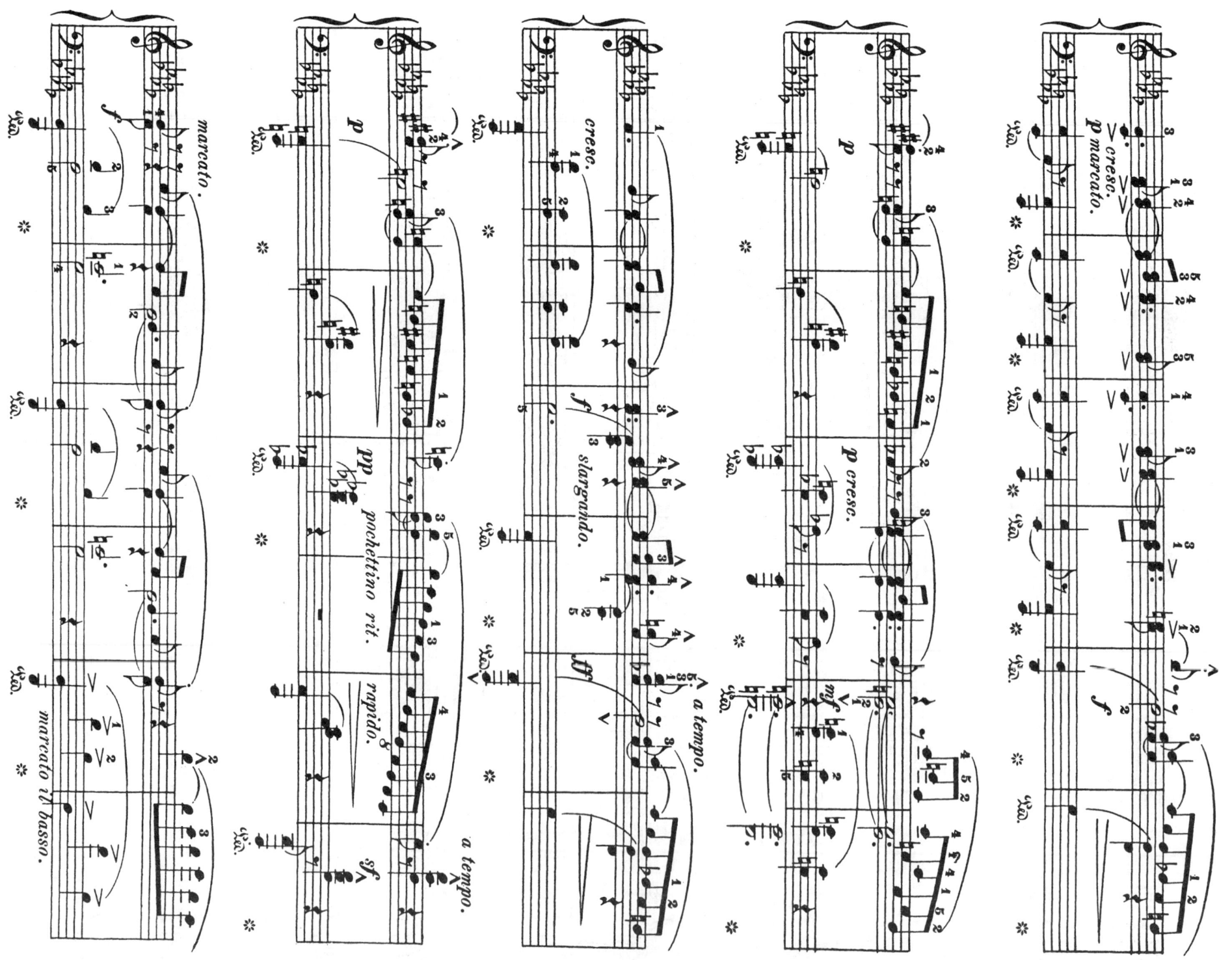

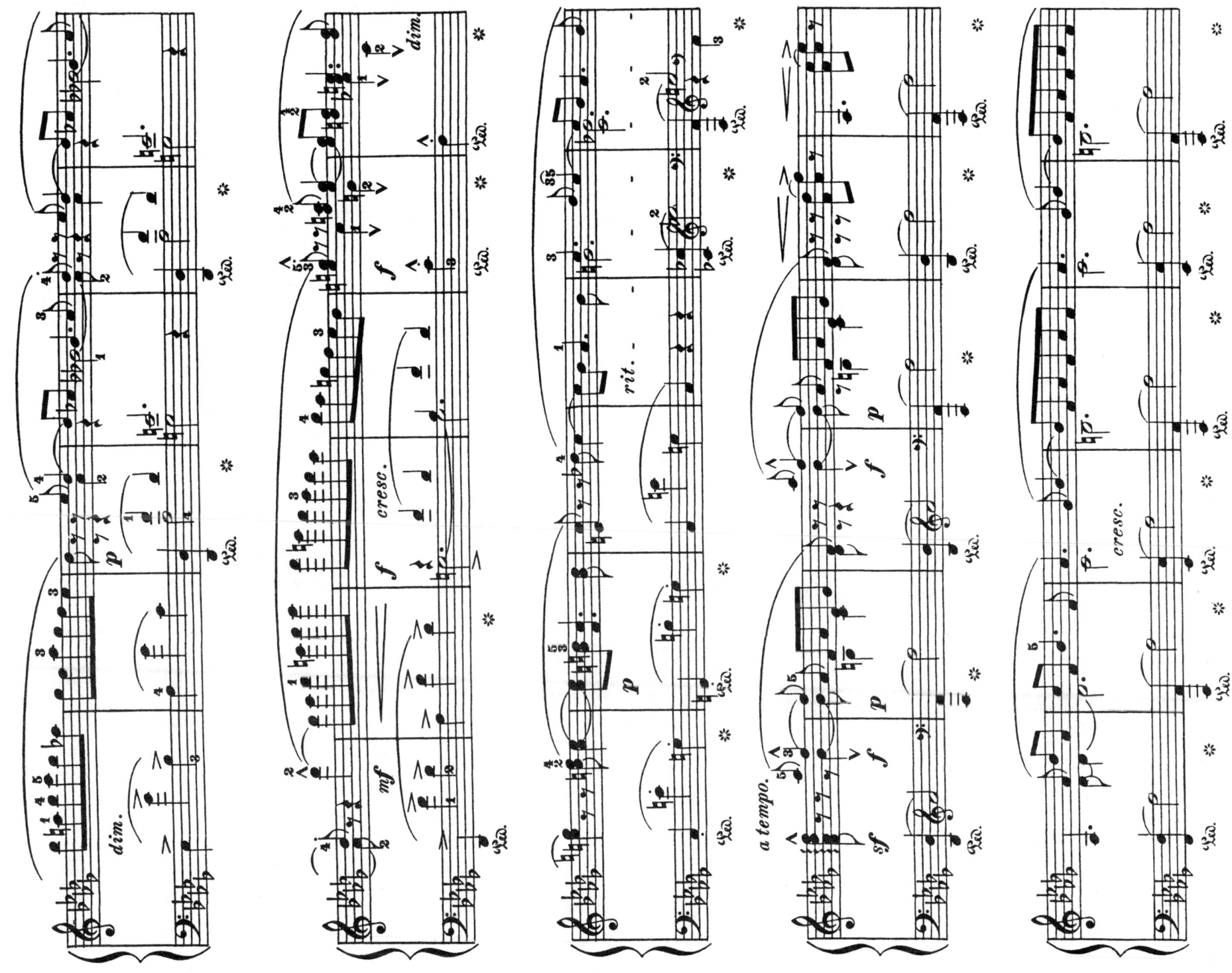

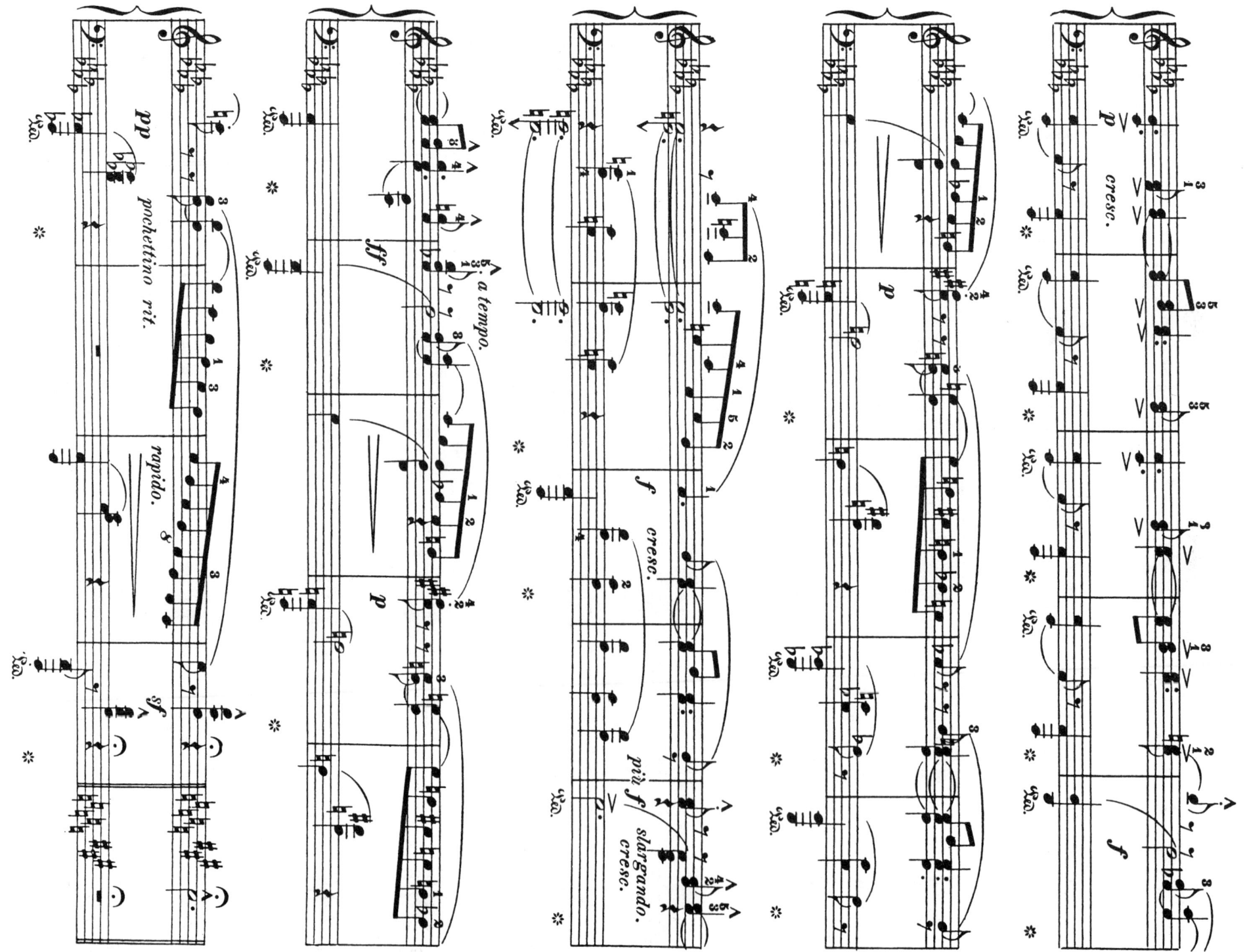

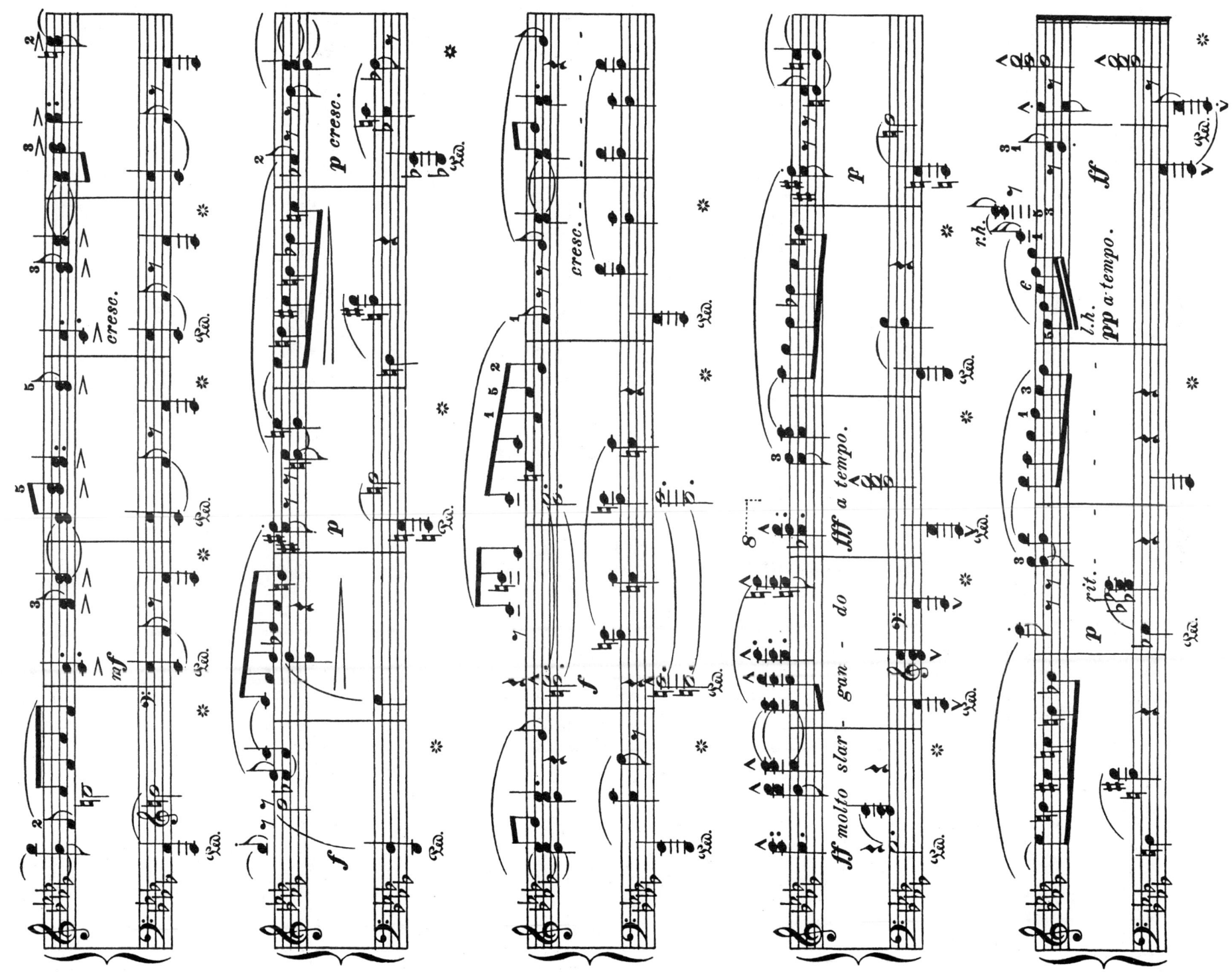

DANSE PASTORALE
Air de Ballet
Opus 37, No. 5

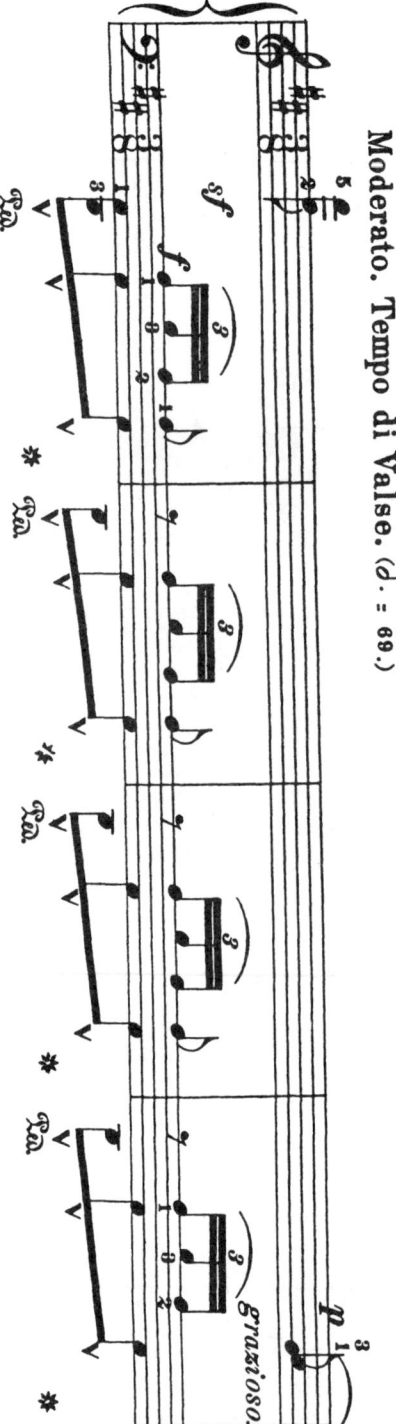

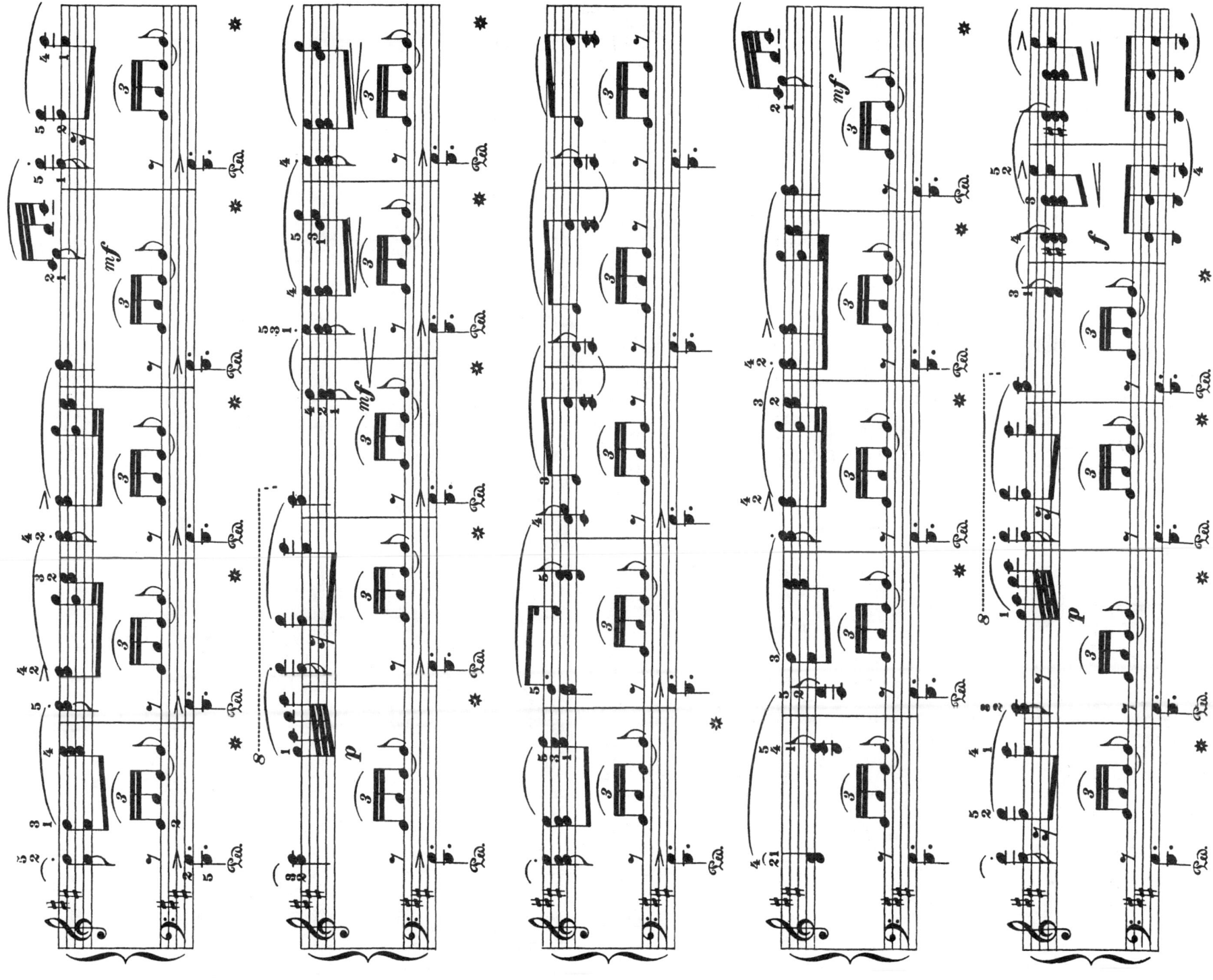

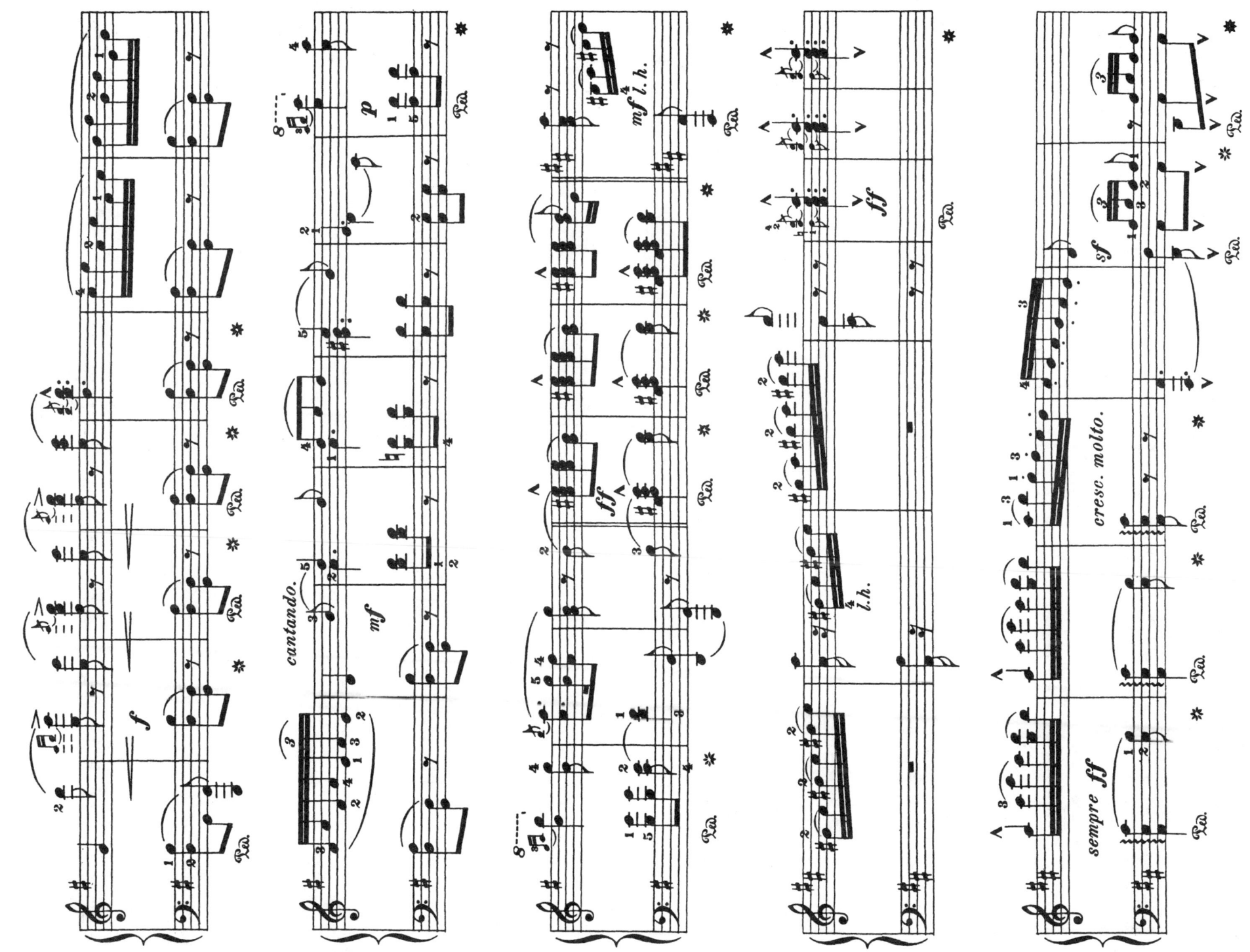

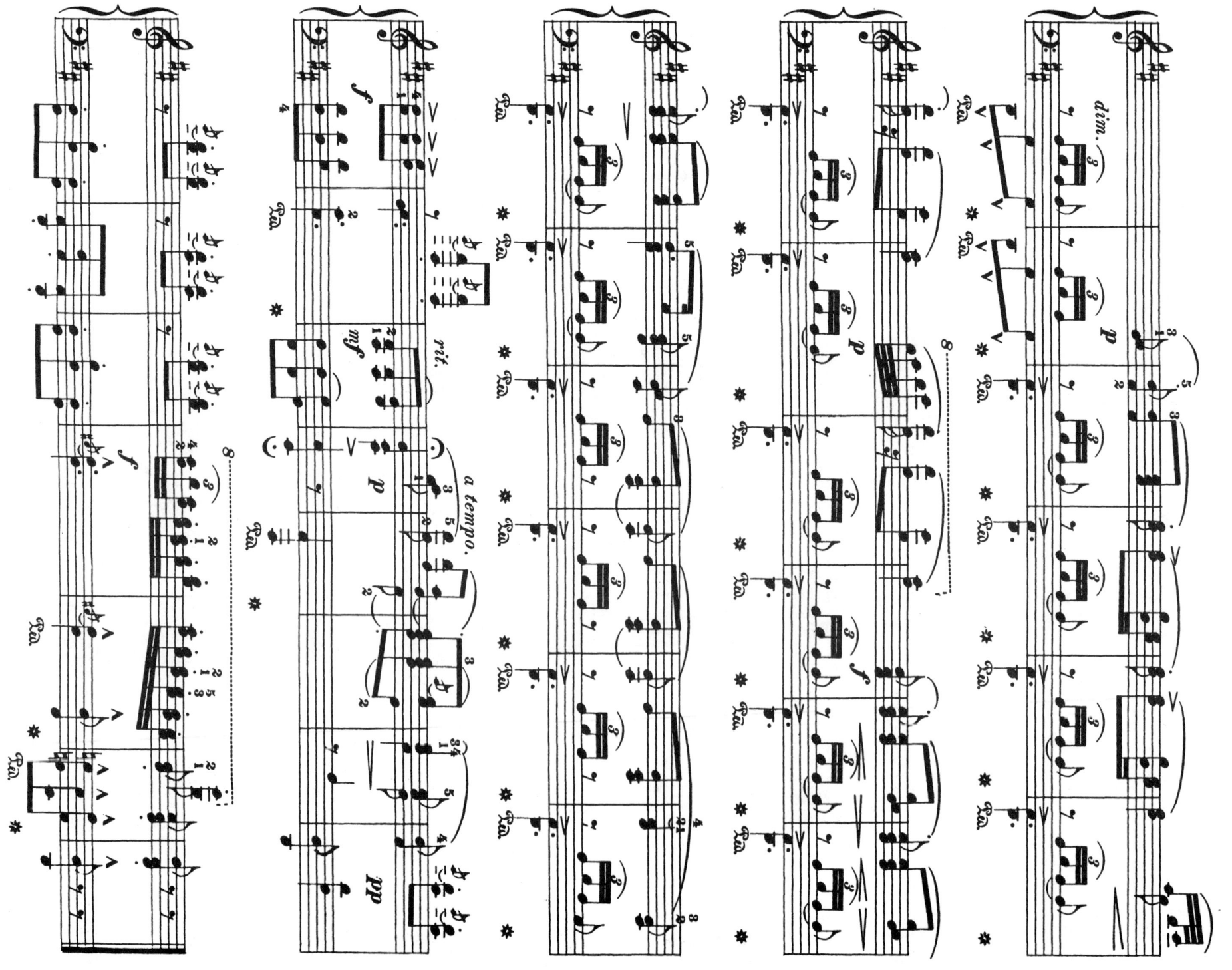

ARLEQUINE
Opus 53

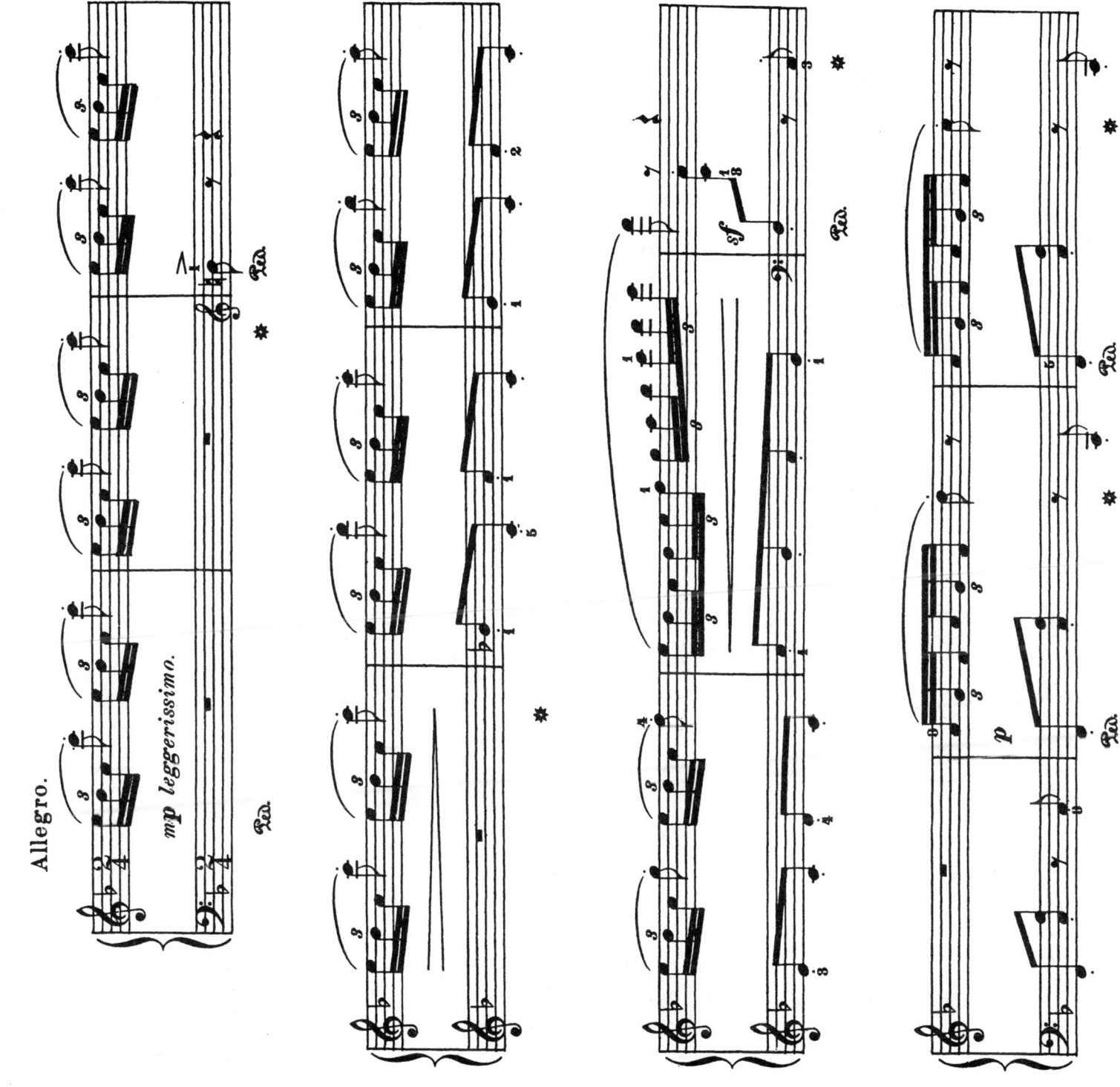

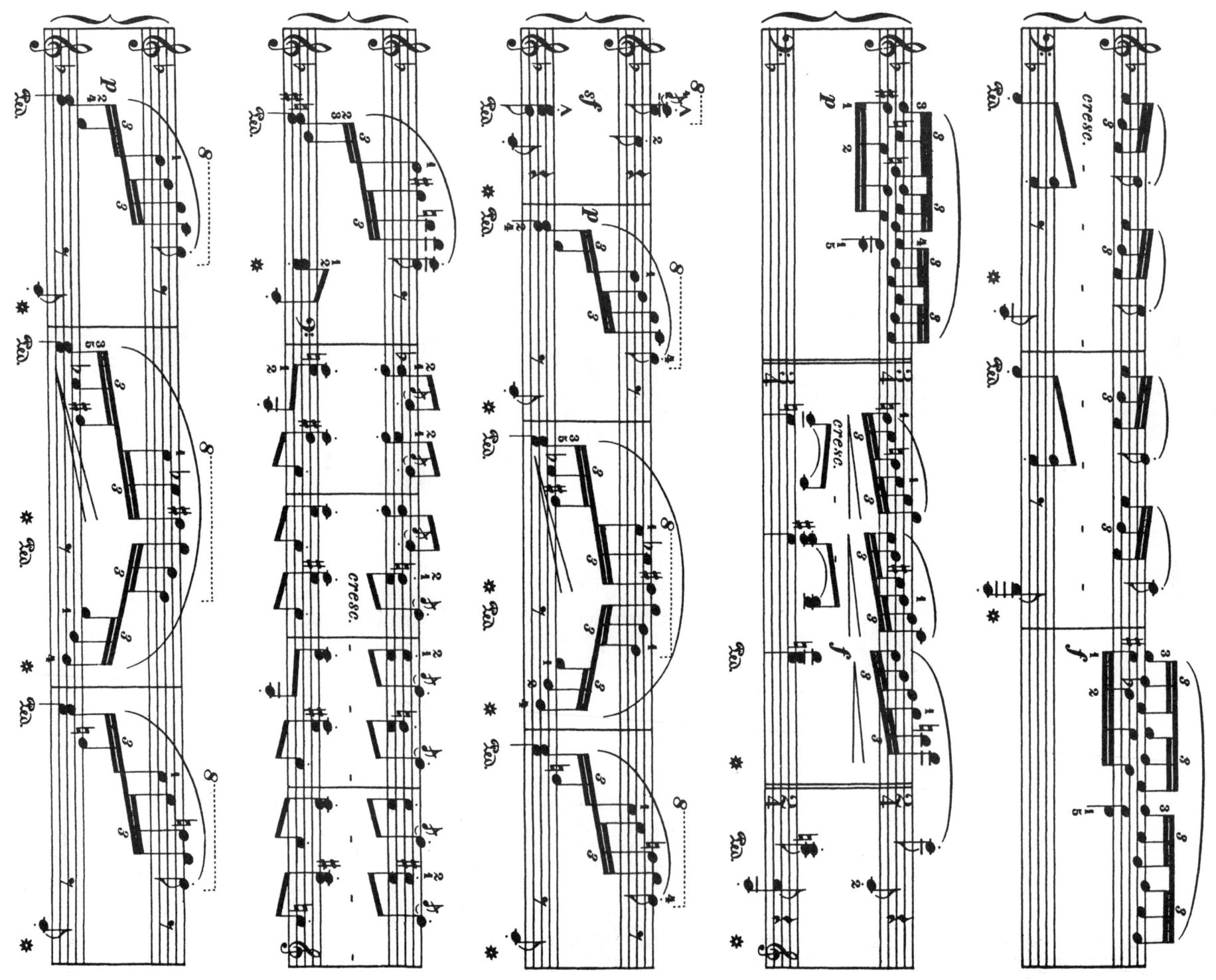

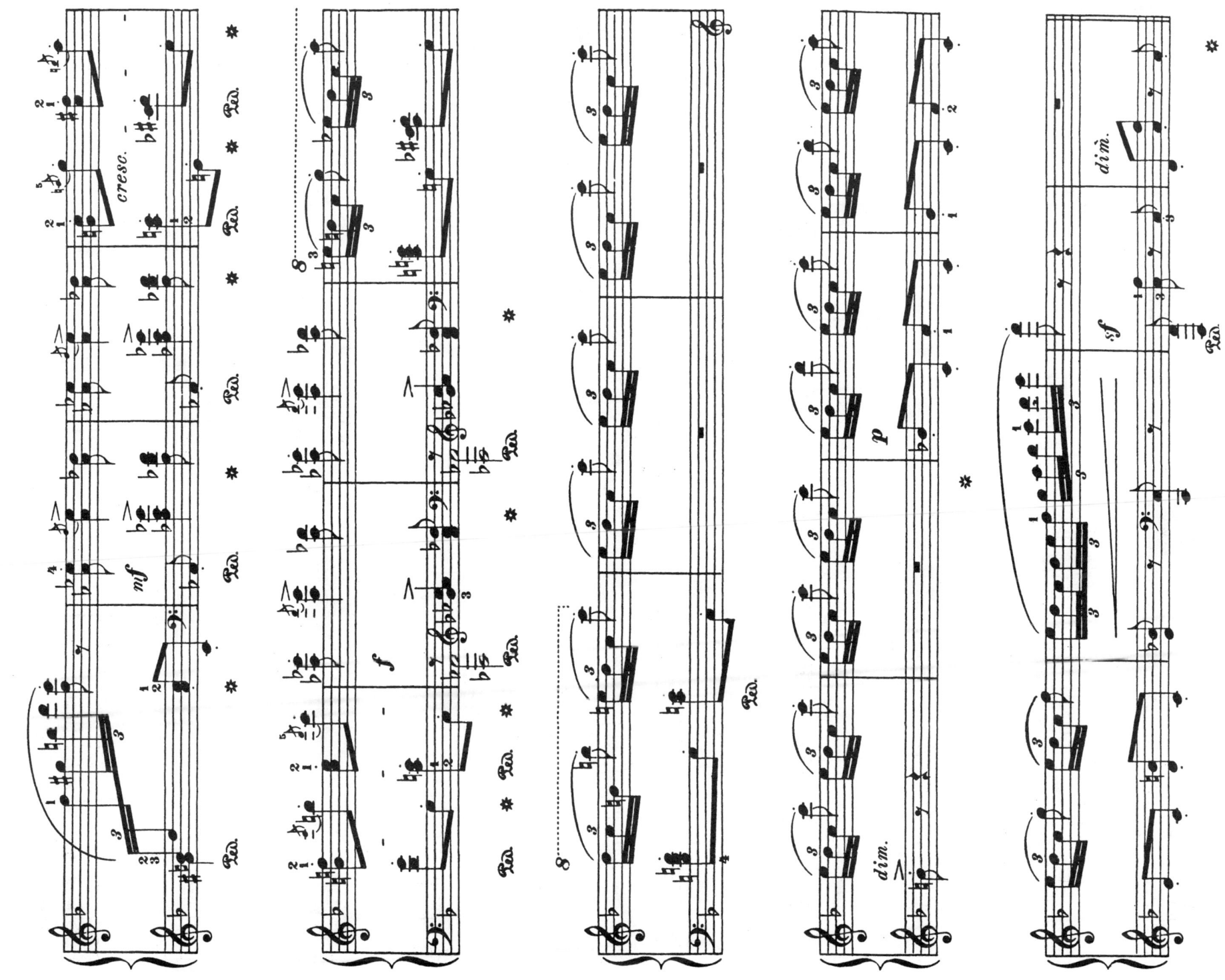

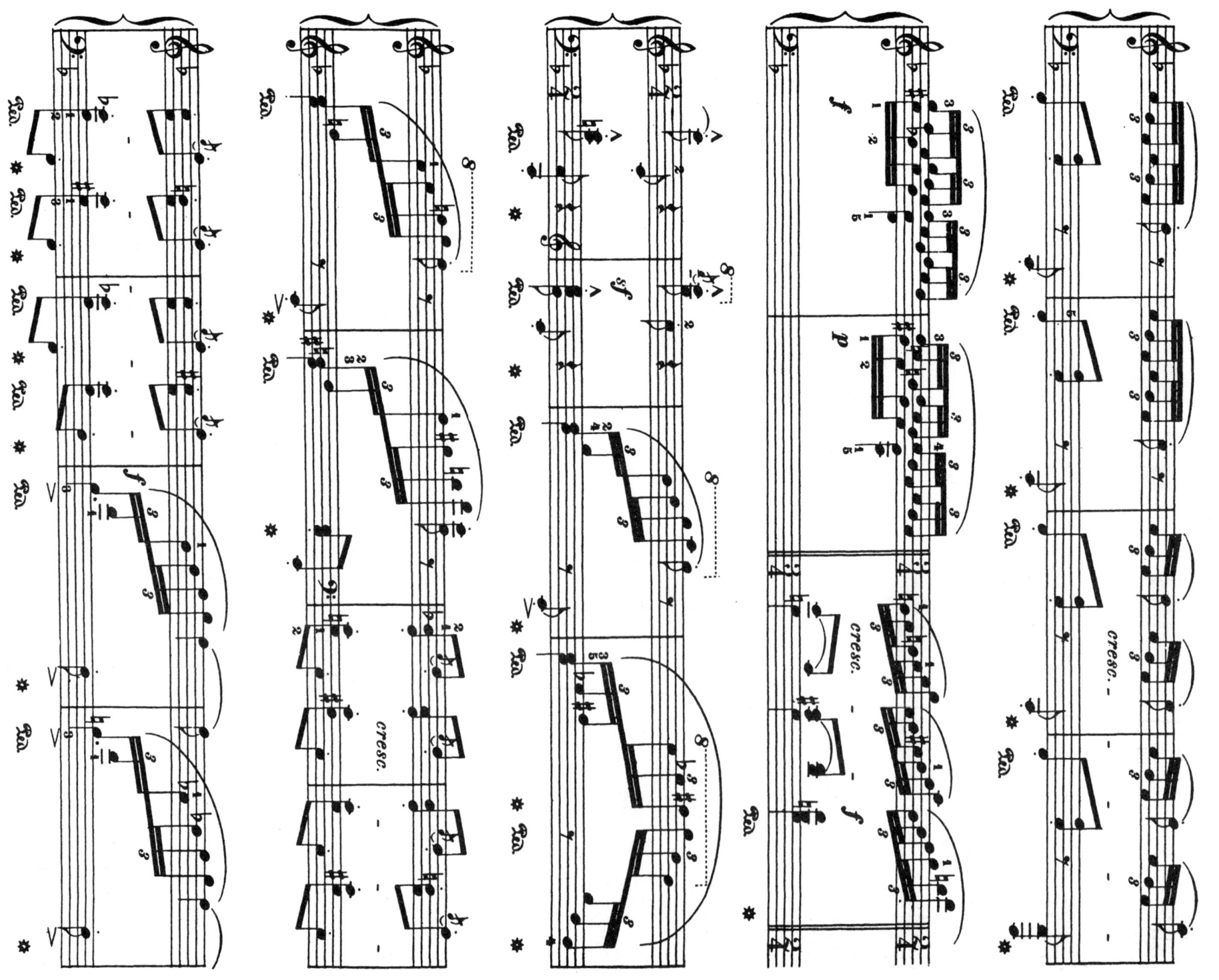

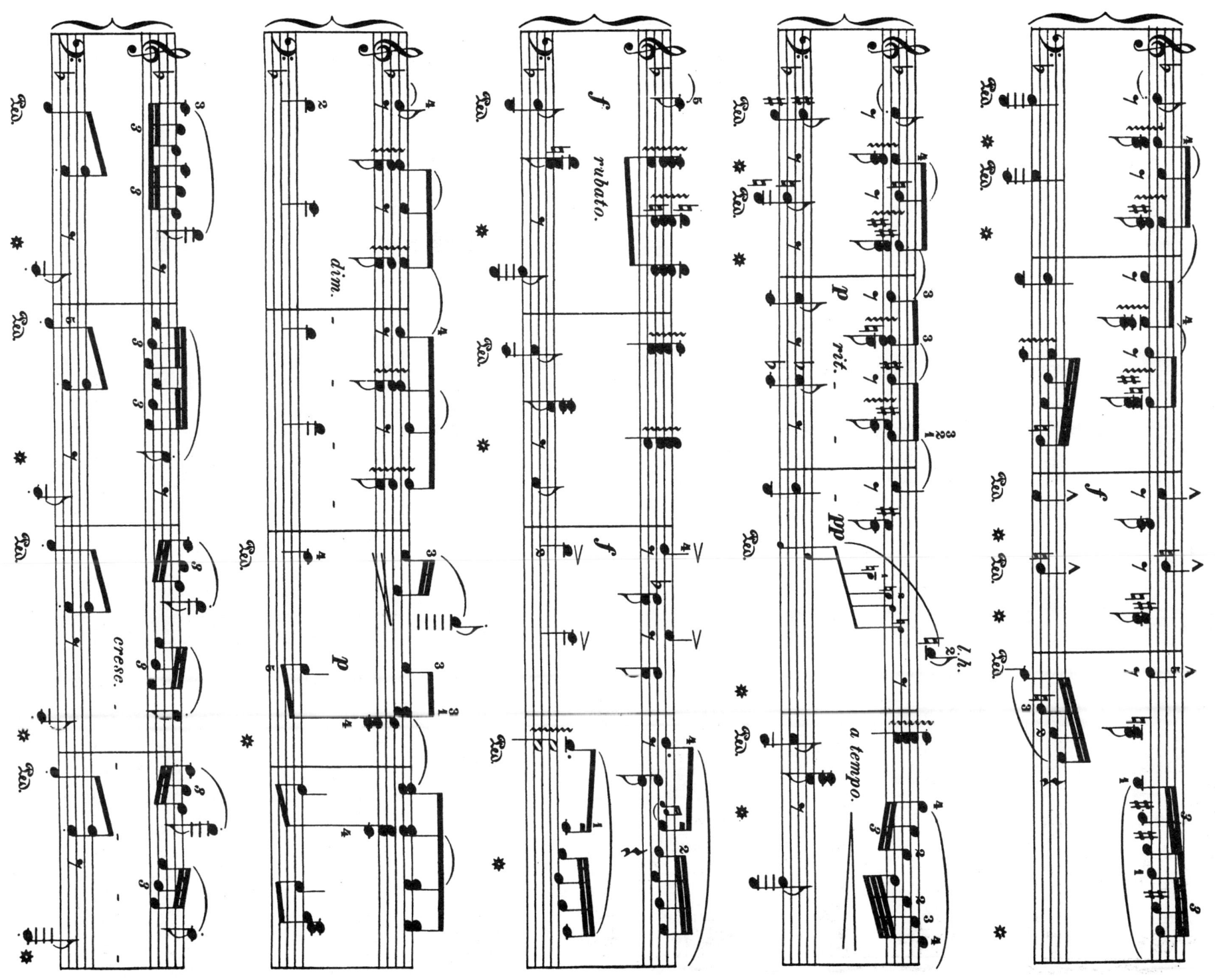

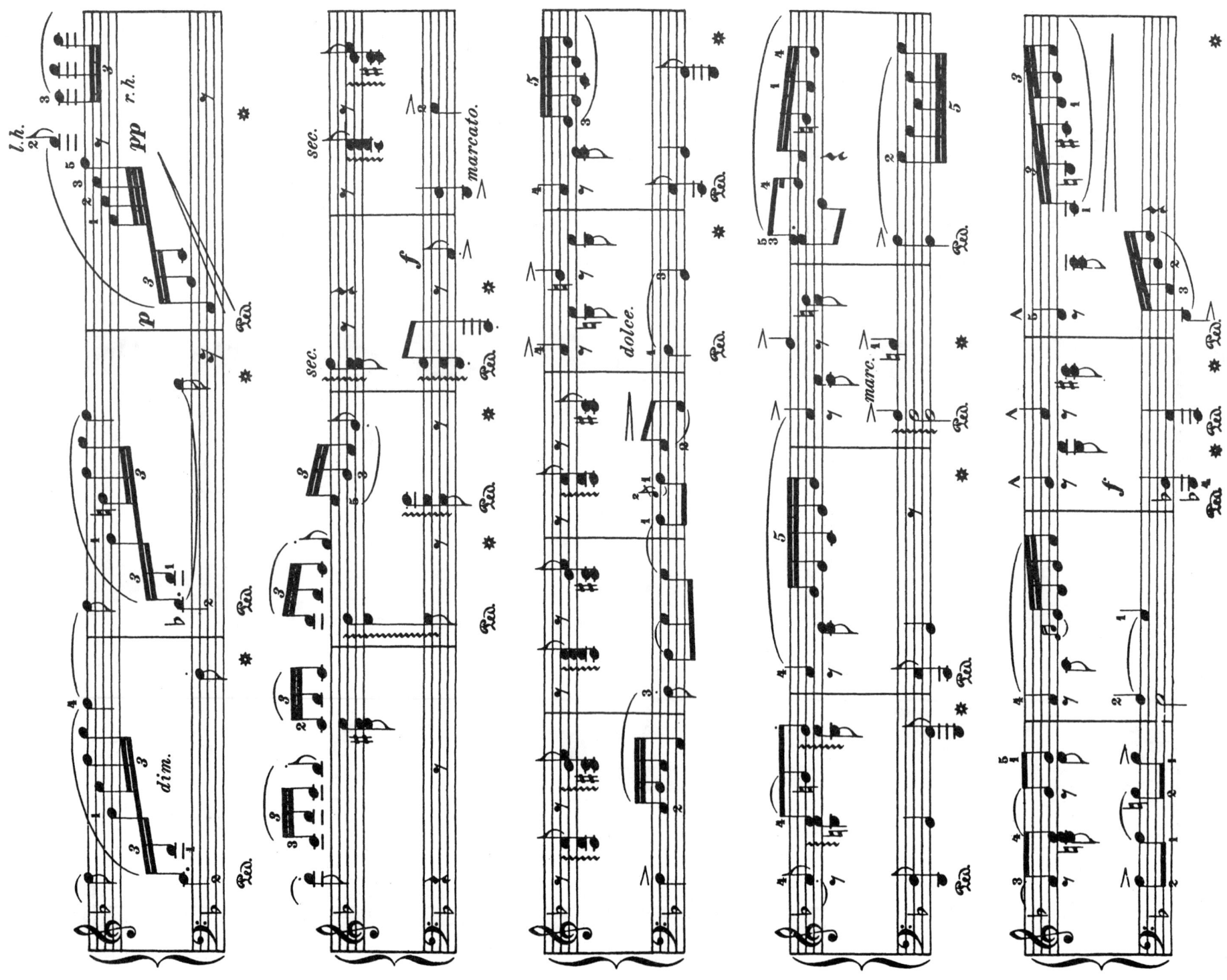

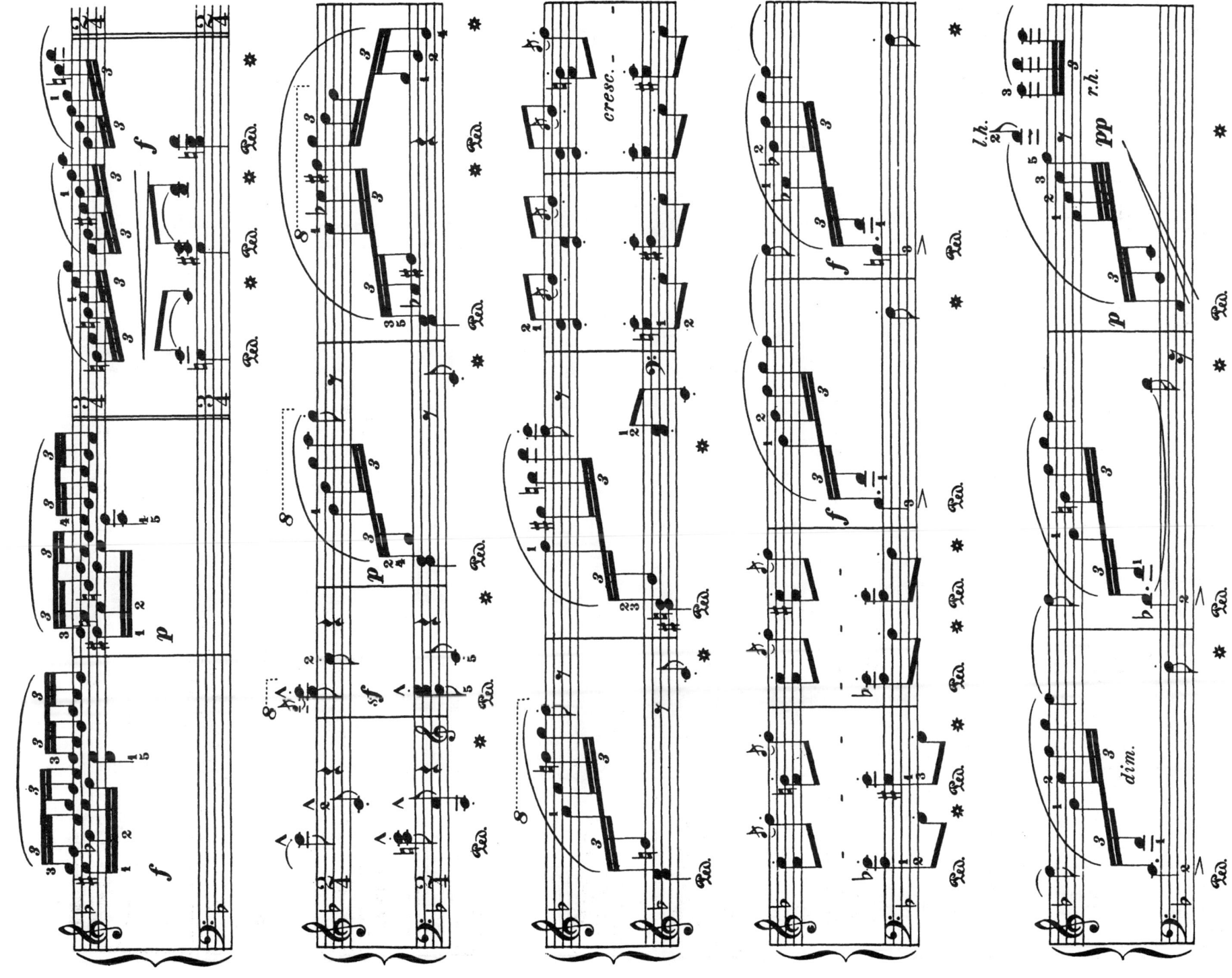

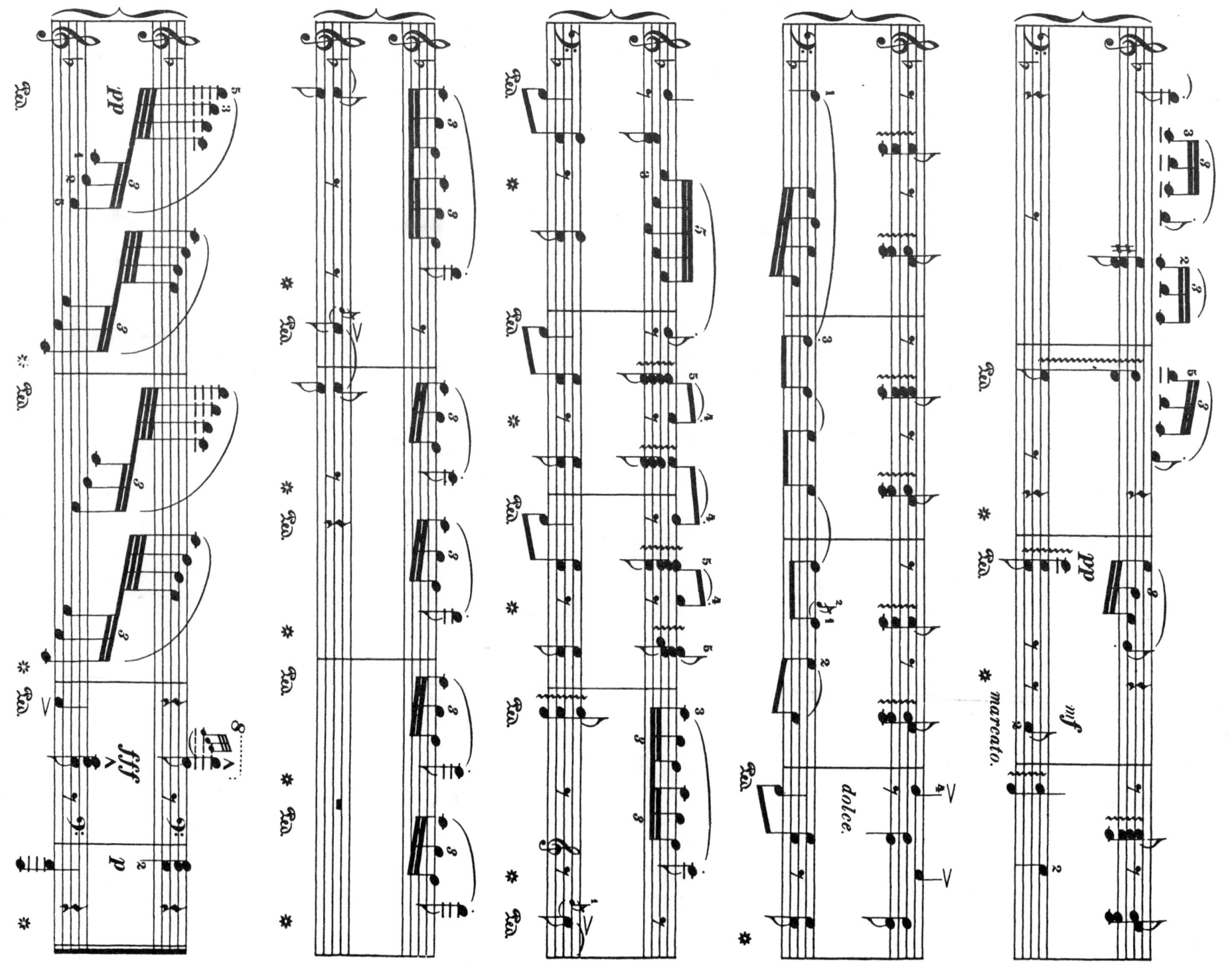